THE RESUME WRITER
Writing It Right

Bernard John Poole

Stephanie Urchick Lashway

Paul W. Layne

Prentice Hall, Englewood Cliffs, NJ 07632

Library of Congress Cataloging-in-Publication Data

Poole, Bernard John.
    The resume writer : writing it right / Bernard John Poole,
Stephanie Urchick Lashway, Paul W. Layne.
      p.   cm.
    Includes bibliographical references (p.   ) and index.
    ISBN 0-13-775388-8
    1. Resumes (Employment) I. Lashway, Stephanie Urchick.
II. Layne, Paul W. III. Title.
HF5383.P66   1992
650.14—dc20   91-10467
                                       CIP

Editorial/production supervision and
  interior design: *Anthony Calcara*
Acquisition editor: *Maureen Hull*
Cover design: *Bruce Kenselaar*
Prepress buyer: *Ilene Levy*
Manufacturing buyer: *Ed O'Dougherty*

© 1992 by Bernard John Poole,
Stephanie Urchick Lashway, Paul W. Layne

Printed in the United States of America

10 9 8 7 6 5 4 3 2 1

ISBN 0-13-775388-8

Prentice-Hall International (UK) Limited, *London*
Prentice-Hall of Australia Pty. Limited, *Sydney*
Prentice-Hall Canada Inc., *Toronto*
Prentice-Hall Hispanoamericana, S.A., *Mexico*
Prentice-Hall of India Private Limited, *New Delhi*
Prentice-Hall of Japan, Inc., *Tokyo*
Simon & Schuster Asia Pte. Ltd., *Singapore*
Editora Prentice-Hall do Brasil, Ltda., *Rio de Janeiro*

Dedication:

For Marilyn, Bob, and Lynne
For our parents, Lucy and William, Virginia and Stephen, and
    Elizabeth and Theodore
And for our students and graduates

Contents

CHAPTER THREE

RESUME CONTENT: THE BUILDING BLOCKS   13

CHAPTER FOUR

ADDITIONAL CATEGORIES OF INFORMATION   22

CHAPTER FIVE

CHOOSING RESUME FORMATS AND LAYOUTS   26

Preface

YOUR RESUME, THE IMPORTANCE OF WRITING IT RIGHT.

Seeking employment is a competitive process that begins with the preparation of an effective resume. This book, and the accompanying software, have been designed to give you an edge on the competition.

A resume and its cover letter are key components in the initial screening of candidates for a job. After all, if you are applying for a position and yours is one among dozens, if not hundreds, of applications, the quality of your resume is all you have going for you. In view of this, it is surprising how often resumes are prepared without consultation and with less than cursory consideration.

Part I will lead you through the process of producing your resume. In its pages you will find advice that works, checklists that will help you produce a quality product, examples of the kinds of resumes that make a difference. You will also find guidance on what to do once you have an effective resume in hand.

After reading Part I, you should be aware that it is impossible for a computer to put together a resume for your special needs without considerable help from you. You need to understand what constitutes a good resume, and how to apply that understanding in support of your own job search. There are many aspects of resume writing that can be facilitated by a computer, but the program has not yet been written which will supply the intelligence and individuality that only you can bring to the task of selling yourself to a prospective employer.

The temptation is usually to reach for the disk and let the computer do the work for you. This is usually a recipe for disaster. Garbage in, garbage out. So take the time to read carefully Part I of THE RESUME WRITER: Writing It Right. Then when you turn to the computer, you will do so with an informed mind. And the computer at the service of an informed mind is a powerful combination.

WHY USE THE RESUME WRITER TO WRITE YOUR RESUME?

The Resume Writer eases the creation of a resume by helping you with subject matter and page layout. Think of the program as a dedicated word processor, dedicated to the task of helping you produce a quality resume.

The Resume Writer simplifies the editing of your resume because, like a word processor, you can change anything anytime with minimal inconvenience.

The Resume Writer gives you flexibility and control by allowing you to customize on the fly to target specific job search needs.

The Resume Writer allows you to save multiple versions on disk, thus assuring you quality reproduction of your customized resumes.

Finally, *The Resume Writer* will teach you how to write a resume. By using the program you will learn the different kinds of resume formats, how to lay out your resume on the page, what kind of data to include, even what vocabulary to use. You can use *The Resume Writer* with confidence, knowing that the end product will effectively serve your needs at this critical first phase of the process of finding a new job.

ACKNOWLEDGMENTS

We are grateful to our colleagues past and present, especially Mr. Mario Cecchetti, Dr. Hubert Callihan, Mr. Ronald Rovansek, Ms. Pier Bocchini, and Mr. Jerry Sheridan for providing an environment in which a project such as this could flourish. But our deepest debt of gratitude must go to our students whose education was the rationale behind the development of the project in the first place.

Hundreds of computer neophytes tested the software, helping us to hone the interface to the point where it is demonstrably easy to use. Through their eyes we were able to appreciate the value of *The Resume Writer* as a tutorial: "It didn't just produce a resume for me—it also taught me *how* to write a resume." From these hundreds of tests we were also able to draw ideas for some of the examples of good resume writing included in the book.

Computer Science majors at The University of Pittsburgh at Johnstown were commissioned to conduct the original analysis and design of the system. They each individually made their respective stabs at implementation. Successive classes designed and implemented enhancements. Many nights' sleep were lost poring over code. And along the way ideas were shared which have contributed to the end product.

Thanks in particular to Matt Smith and Alan Hoberney for the special impact they made on the project. Our students will, indeed, continue to make a contribution, since *The Resume Writer's* longevity will depend on the ingenuity of future generations of nascent Software Engineers.

A final word of thanks must go to the reviewers of the manuscript whose suggestions greatly improved the structure of the text. Thanks also to Liz Kendall, Jane Baumann, and, more especially, Maureen Hull at Prentice-Hall whose guidance and encouragement were greatly appreciated, especially during the later stages of the project.

THE ART OF WRITING
A RESUME

chapter 1

Resumes and the World of Work

LEARNING OBJECTIVES:

After reading the chapter you will have an understanding of what a resume is and what it can do for you in your job search. In particular you will learn about the following topics:

- Resumes and the world of work
- Resume: What is it?
- Resume: Who prepares it?
- Resume: When and Why do you need one?
- Resume: Where does it fit in your employment search?
- Resume: How do you create it?

1.1 RESUMES AND THE WORLD OF WORK

In today's job market, it is a rare applicant who does not have to produce a resume as a tool for the employment search. Because of the variety of jobs now available, and because of the numbers of people currently seeking work, employers use the resume as an initial screening device. By reviewing an applicant's resume, the employer can quickly tell whether or not a candidate has something to contribute to the organization. A glance down the page shows the employer the blend of experience, education, skills, and abilities that the potential employee can bring to the company.

Stop reading for a moment and think about the last television commercial you can remember or the last magazine advertisement you can recall.

Commercials and ads both attempt to convince an audience that a product or service is worth buying or trying. Why do you suppose you remembered that particular commercial? Was it promoting a product or service that you happened to need? Did that magazine ad appeal to you on a visual level? An emotional one? Did the advertisers convince you that the item or service was something that worked? Was it something that you had to have? Was it something you would not be sorry you purchased? If the marketers did their jobs correctly, they convinced you of the product's value and you probably did end up trying or buying the merchandise. (Unless, of course, you simply were not able to make a purchase at the time.)

A good resume is no different from an effective television commercial or magazine advertisement. If you do the job correctly, if you **Write it Right**, you will convince employers that you are a valuable candidate worth trying. (Unless they are not able to make a hire at that particular time!)

The software that accompanies this book, THE RESUME WRITER, will work hand in hand with the text as your advertising consultant. Use them in conjunction with one another to help make a strong presentation of your qualities and skills to prospective employees.

1.2   RESUME: WHAT IS IT?

The French word **résumé**[1] means a summary, a brief, an outline. Resumes are exactly that—brief and merely a summary of you. If you were to write everything about everything you have ever done, you would end up with a book, not a resume.

The other reason your resume must be brief is that an employer will spend only a brief amount of time reviewing it. It is estimated that employers average about 20 seconds reading each resume. If you submit a document that is too lengthy, an employer may get "turned off" before even beginning to read. Twenty seconds does not sound like a fair or reasonable amount of time to review your resume, but that is the time required to find out if you have the background the company is looking for.

This is why THE RESUME WRITER allows you no more than six lines for any of the items in your resume. You could no doubt write pages of useful information for some sections, such as your previous employment experience. But which Personnel Office staff has time to read so much, especially when there are perhaps two hundred other applicants whose resumes must also be reviewed? By limiting you to six lines, THE RESUME WRITER is encouraging you to think about what you write, encouraging you to include only those summary details that will make a lasting impression on the reader.

It is important to remember that a resume will not get you a job—the only purpose of a well-written resume is to get you to an interview. A resume is the important first step in your job search.

1.3   RESUME: WHO PREPARES IT?

A most important lesson to learn is that you and you alone must create your resume. There are many people out there who would like to take your money to

---

[1] The accents are necessary in French, but are usually omitted in English.

produce "the perfect resume" for you. The reality is that these people can do nothing **unless you provide the basic information**. Resume writing services simply take the data you supply and format it. The end result is a professional looking document, but was it really worth $95 (or even more) for something you can create yourself?

Nobody knows you like you do. Take the time to do a self-inventory before you begin this resume-writing project. Use the outline offered at the beginning of THE RESUME WRITER to prepare a rough draft of your resume. List your experiences, accomplishments, things you know how to do, activities or hobbies you enjoy, places you have travelled to, and so on. Not all of this information will appear on every resume you write, but having this list will help you choose what to say to which audiences.

Your resume changes with time, just as you do. And it changes, too, depending on what kind of company will be reading it, what kind of job you will be looking for, etc. THE RESUME WRITER is special in this respect, too, because it allows you to easily create different versions of your resume (see Chapter Nine).

You will notice when you produce your resume using THE RESUME WRITER that you will be able to choose your own format for parts of the resume. This will allow you to personalize the appearance of the resume, and thus improve its effectiveness.

Interestingly enough, most people use the same resume for all job applications. The reason is simple: producing one version was difficult enough without the help of THE RESUME WRITER. The idea of tailoring each resume to focus on the varied requirements of each application is usually resisted because it is more trouble and time than it is worth.

However, when you use THE RESUME WRITER, such flexibility becomes the rule rather than the exception. As explained above, you have complete control over your resume. You can change objectives, references, relevant work experience, relevant education, relevant honors, relevant activities, relevant anything, without needing to rewrite the entire resume.

Moreover, you can save as many versions of your resume as you want. In this day and age, the likelihood of your carrying out a job search every few years is greatly increased by the rapid pace of change both in the work place as well as in society at large. How convenient it would be if the various versions of your resume that you created two, three, or four years back were available to you once again. All you would need to do would be to update your resume using the EDIT function of THE RESUME WRITER, as explained in Chapter Eleven.

1.4   RESUME: WHEN AND WHY DO YOU NEED ONE?

When you need a resume and why you need a resume are closely related. Anytime you are seeking employment, either a first job, a new job, or a career change, you will be required to create a document outlining your experience and qualifications—a resume.

The most significant reason you need a resume is that employers require one—and that should be reason enough. But a second reason you need to produce a resume is that putting yourself down on paper is a good way for you to assess your background, your strengths, your weak areas, your skills, your abilities, your temperament. This makes it much easier to plan your career moves and to promote yourself to prospective employers.

1.5   RESUME: WHERE DOES IT FIT IN YOUR EMPLOYMENT SEARCH?

Where you submit your resume and what else you do with it will depend on your particular job search strategies. Certainly you will want to submit copies to prospective employers, either through a mail campaign or by delivering them personally. The advantage of a mail campaign is that by using directories and lists, you will be able to target hundreds of companies who could use your skills. The disadvantage is that many of those companies may not have a need at the time for someone with your background, and most of them will not even acknowledge receipt of your resume.

The advantage of delivering resumes personally to companies is that in some cases you may actually get an opportunity to meet the person with the hiring power. A resume delivered by a candidate who is appropriately dressed and eager to make a good first impression may be even more effective than one that is received by mail. After all, a resume is simply a piece of paper and has no personality. But if you approach organizations directly, and act in a polished, professional way, you will add that same polished professionalism to the document you submit.

There are two disadvantages to delivering your resumes in person. Firstly, you will be limited geographically, financially, and physically in the number of companies you can target. Secondly, there will be times when you will not be able to meet with a personnel representative or a person with the power to hire. You may only be able to leave your resume with a secretary or you may be told that the company is simply not accepting applications or resumes at the time.

Resumes can also be submitted to employment agencies, to organizations that produce books of resumes, or to electronic resume services.* You should also give copies of your resume to individuals who may be asked to supply a recommendation for you (references, former co-workers or employers) and to the people in your networking system (relatives, professional acquaintances, personal contacts). More details on what to do with your resume appear in Chapter 8.

1.6   RESUME: HOW DO YOU CREATE IT?

The remaining question in your resume development is "How do I create this document?" Let us consider again those marketers who create the commercials and advertisements that seem to work best. There are two questions that they must ask and answer before setting up any campaign: What am I trying to sell? To whom am I trying to sell it? What and Who. Product/service and audience.

This is the same approach you need to take before beginning to create your resume. Ask yourself, "What am I trying to sell and to whom am I trying to sell it?" In other words, what kind of job am I looking for and what companies would be interested in me? Your resume is your commercial. Any good salesperson will tell you that it is impossible to try to sell something to someone if you don't know *what* you are selling or *to whom* you are selling. You will only create an effective resume if you first know what you want to do in the labor

---

*These latter are companies that put your resume into a database that is online to the telephone network. This means that it can be accessed using a computer by any other organization that subscribes to the electronic resume service company. Thus, when a need arises to fill a position the organization can, at the speed of a telephone call, acquire copies of the resumes of all those candidates whose skills match the organization's job requirements.

market; and second have some idea of the type of employers who would be interested in your services.

Your plan for marketing yourself in the world of work must begin with a sound occupational objective. If you have a difficult time identifying what type of work you want to do, or if you aren't sure what type of work is available for someone with your background, your first step will involve research. Use the local library, visit the area bureau of employment security, check local college and university career centers. Ask questions. Ask for referrals to other sources of information.

You must know what it is you are looking for before you begin your resume. You must also know what type of organizations you will be targeting in your employment search.

These are important answers for you to have. You should also have some general guidelines about putting yourself down on paper. When you create your resume using THE RESUME WRITER you will "learn by doing" what an effective resume contains in terms of information, and how it should be laid out on the page. The next chapter puts THE RESUME WRITER in context by giving answers to some of the most commonly asked questions regarding resumes.

chapter 2

What's In and What's Out— Resume Writing Guidelines

LEARNING OBJECTIVES:

This chapter explores some commonly asked questions regarding resume preparation. Myths and realities are reviewed and you will have answers to queries on:

- Resume Writing Guidelines
  - Length
  - Objective statements
  - Personal data entries
  - Use of photographs
  - General or specific content
  - Color and quality of paper
  - Gimmicks vs. creativity
  - Salary history, reasons for separations, negative information
  - References
  - Preferred styles, formats, and readability

2.1 RESUME WRITING GUIDELINES

Resumes have been around for a number of years now, and so have stories about candidates' resumes that employers find to be effective, ineffective, or amusing. Although there exists a certain individualism when it comes to preferences, most employers and others who screen resumes agree on general guidelines for creating the document. The following topics are among the most frequently discussed resume writing items.

2.1.1 LENGTH

Because the resume is a personal commercial, you can expect a reader to spend about the same amount of time reading your resume as it takes to watch a commercial—approximately 20 seconds. If you submit a document that is too lengthy, or too wordy, the reader may lose interest before even beginning to read. It is recommended that a resume should be one page if you are a recent graduate with limited experience. If your background includes a wider diversity or number of experiences, you may need to extend your resume to a page and a half. Applicants to institutions of higher education are required to submit more detailed information (publications, presentations, courses taught, seminars attended), and in those cases this rule does not apply.

Unless you are applying for positions in higher education, keep your resume to one page and a half or less.

2.1.2 OBJECTIVE STATEMENTS

Most recruiters indicate that the occupational objective should be included in a resume if you are new to the work world and do not have an established career field and track record. What you are interested in doing for a company may not always be clear by the title of your educational degree or title of your last position, especially if you have a liberal arts background, a varied work experience, or are interested in changing careers. Since cover letters may remain in a personnel office while a resume is routed to departments with hiring needs, it will not be enough to have your occupational desires only in your accompanying letter.

Unless your general career direction has been confirmed by experience, include a specific statement of your occupational objective on a resume.

2.1.3 PERSONAL DATA ENTRIES

Information other than your name, addresses, and telephone numbers is usually considered unimportant. A resume stresses your skills and accomplishments. Age, height, physical condition, marital status, and so on, do not reflect your ability to do a job unless you are applying for positions such as a television reporter, model, weight trainer, or travelling salesperson. Although this information typically appears on job application forms, it is not considered to be a valuable resume entry.

THE RESUME WRITER does not, therefore, offer an opportunity to include such data in a traditional chronological resume, since it is the exception rather than the rule. If you consider yourself an exception, then these details can still be included in your cover letter, which you can read more about in Chapter Seven. Alternatively, you can use one of the two other formats, either the functional or the combination format, which provide an opportunity for more extensive use of freeform sections. Read Chapter Five to find out more about these alternatives.

Personal information should be limited to name, addresses, and telephone numbers unless directly related to a job requirement.

2.1.4 USE OF PHOTOGRAPHS

A picture may be worth a thousand words, but including one on your resume is not recommended. Using photographs on resumes was a popular thing to do as late as the 1970's. Today it is considered a space waster. Some states may prohibit photographs by law, so even applicants for media, modelling, and acting careers need to be wary. Inclusion of a photo should directly relate to a BFOQ (Bona Fide Occupational Qualification).

Do not include a personal photograph on a resume.

2.1.5 GENERAL OR SPECIFIC CONTENT

Employers want to know exactly what you can do for them. Be specific. Give examples and use quantifiers (how many? how much?) to help a reader understand your skills and abilities. Keep in mind, though, that not everyone who reads your resume, especially an initial screener, will understand extremely technical language. Keep jargon, technical or otherwise, to a minimum.

Use specific examples and information on your resume to explain your skills and competencies.

2.1.6 COLOR AND QUALITY OF PAPER

Almost twenty years ago, job seekers began trying to stand out from the competition by submitting resumes produced on either blue, green, pink, or some other "non-white" color. Of course, the effectiveness of this ploy has worn off and recruiters have ended up with a rainbow of paper to review. Business and the world of work is conservative, and most employers agree that white or off-white shades are the appropriate color choices for resumes and cover letters.

The quality of paper preferred has never changed. Medium weight and polished linen, rag, or bond texture will provide a professional appearance and quality to your resume.

A paper of good quality weight, texture, and a white or off-white color will produce the most professional-looking resume.

2.1.7 GIMMICKS VERSUS CREATIVITY

When a labor market gets tight, some job seekers will resort to whatever it takes to get noticed. A story was recently circulated about a recruiter who received a box in the mail and opened it to find a man's shoe with a resume printed on the sole. Attached was a note saying, "I just wanted to get my foot in the door." Another candidate, trying desperately to be interviewed at a particular company, sent a different gift to the personnel office each week (candy, flowers, balloons, gourmet food), with his resume enclosed. While such gimmicks may evoke a laugh or two, in the conservatism of business, such tricks seldom impress employers.

Some fields, such as graphic communications or advertising, place a premium on creativity. Job seekers in these careers have more leeway in diverging from the standard, basic resume formats. Good taste and good judgment, however, remain the foundation for divergence.

Use gimmicks cautiously as they may evoke negative responses from employers. Be creative, but use good taste and judgment.

2.1.8 SALARY HISTORY, REASONS FOR LEAVING JOBS, NEGATIVE INFORMATION

No mention of past salaries received or salary desired should appear on a resume. Listing past compensations may exclude you from consideration before you have a fighting chance if your salaries were higher or lower than what is typical. It may also be interpreted that you are overly concerned about salary, instead of the responsibilities and rewards of a career.

Why you left an organization should not be included in your employment entries. It is another space waster, and will be discussed at an interview anyway. Any information which may be construed in a negative way should not appear on a resume. Only information that supports your candidacy, i.e. skills, abilities, achievements, and so on should be used.

This is not to say you should be dishonest. During interviews and on employment applications you will have opportunities to report and discuss areas you must bring to the company's attention. Resumes, remember, are personal commercials. You only have a short amount of time to highlight the best parts of your presentation.

Do not include salary information, reasons for leaving jobs, or other information which is not directly related to your skills and abilities.

2.1.9 REFERENCES

Employers know that everyone can find folks who will say wonderful things about them. (You're in serious trouble if you can't.) Checking references is a second or third step after an employer has determined that you can do the job. It is assumed that references are available upon request, but you may choose to include that statement at the end of your resume.

If an employer has specifically asked for references to be included with a resume or initial application letter, then choose two or three individuals (not related) who can comment on your ability to work, and your ability to learn. A suggestion would be former professors and former employers. Ask in advance if they are willing to serve as a reference for you, and notify them if there have been changes in your name, career objective, etc.

THE RESUME WRITER does allow you to include references in your resume because sometimes this is a requirement in employment ads. You may, of course, choose to leave this blank. However, when there is room on the printed page at the end of your resume, THE RESUME WRITER will append the standard phrase: "References available upon request."

References are not usually included on a resume.

2.1.10 PREFERRED STYLES, FORMATS, AND READABILITY

There seems to be no strong preference among employers as to format and style (more on formats and styles in Chapter 5). They do have strong feelings, though, about the proper use of grammar, spelling, and the use of white space and headings to make resumes easy to read. Chronological resumes with a traditional or basic layout appear to be most widely used, and therefore most widely recognized as appropriate.

Employers are not as concerned with format and style as they are with ease of reading and error-free documents.

Chapters Three to Eight present more detailed information about the ten topics discussed in this chapter. Now that you have some general guidelines to follow, it's time to build that resume!

chapter 3

Resume Content:
The Building Blocks

LEARNING OBJECTIVES:

After reading this chapter you will know the four fundamental categories of information that form the foundation of any resume document you will prepare:

- □ Resume building blocks
  - □ Including personal information
  - □ Defining employment objectives
  - □ Listing educational background
  - □ Highlighting employment experiences
    - □ Paid work experience
    - □ Unpaid work experience

3.1 RESUME BUILDING BLOCKS

There are four basic categories of information that a reader will want to see on your resume. These include a personal section, an occupational objective, and entries describing educational and/or employment experiences. Although each individual employer will be looking for different sets of credentials and skills, these entries are the "building blocks"—the foundation—on which you will base your resume presentation.

Even if you choose a format other than chronological, it is a good idea to complete these entries so that you have a written record of the skills and training you possess and how you have used them professionally. In the event you do choose another type of resume format (such as for a functional resume), this information may not appear exactly as described below.

THE RESUME WRITER allows you to choose from one of three different formats:

- The traditional Chronological format, which is designed to describe your educational and work experience in reverse chronological order;
- The Functional format, which is appropriate when you want to focus on *what you can do* in terms of the professional and personal skills you can bring to a job, rather than on *what you have done;*
- The hybrid Combination format which, as its name implies, is a cross between the two basic types of resume.

Which of these three types to use is not always an easy decision. Chapter Five will help you decide which is best for you.

3.2   INCLUDING PERSONAL INFORMATION

The first item listed on your resume should be your name, address or addresses, and telephone numbers (see Fig 3-1). Additional personal data, if you choose to include it, should appear in a later category. Be sure to include a telephone number, even if it is a number where messages can be taken for you. Employers are very busy people and will usually not consider writing to you concerning an interview appointment. In fact, "serious" job hunters invest in telephone answering machines so as not to miss calls from prospective employers. A campus, or other temporary, address should be so noted.

```
Calvin N. Pittman

Home Address:               Present Address:
146 Ginger Avenue           987 Binns Hall
Johnstown, PA 15904         California, PA 15419
(814) 266-9999              (412) 938-9999
```

Figure 3-1   *Personal contact information.*

3.3   DEFINING EMPLOYMENT OBJECTIVES

Right after reading who you are, employers want to know what it is you want to do for them. (By now this should sound very familiar.) Many job seekers object to including employment goals on the resume fearing that it might limit them to the occupational area they have listed.

This is precisely the point of including goals. Because of the volume of resumes received, both solicited and unsolicited, employers want to know quickly what it is that the applicant is interested in doing for the company. If your employment goals match a need the company has for hiring, the reader is likely to continue reviewing your resume. On the other hand, if your objectives do not match the company's needs at that time, or if you fail to include your employment objectives, you may simply be filed for future consideration.

Writing an employment objective may be the most difficult part of constructing your resume. A goal statement should be brief, no more than 20–30 words. It should also be clear and meaningful. Many job seekers have fallen into the trap of using clichés found in resume guides and manuals. A statement such as:

"To pursue a career within a growth-oriented organization that will allow me to contribute to the company while fulfilling my own personal occupational expectations."

says absolutely nothing to an employer.

When writing the employment objective you may choose several ways to explain your goals (Fig. 3-2). One way is simply to list an occupational designation such as:

"Seeking a position as a registered nurse."

or

"Design engineer—three-dimensional CADD operations."

Another method involves listing a functional area and a specific environment.

"Seeking entry-level management position, preferably in food service establishment or supermarket."

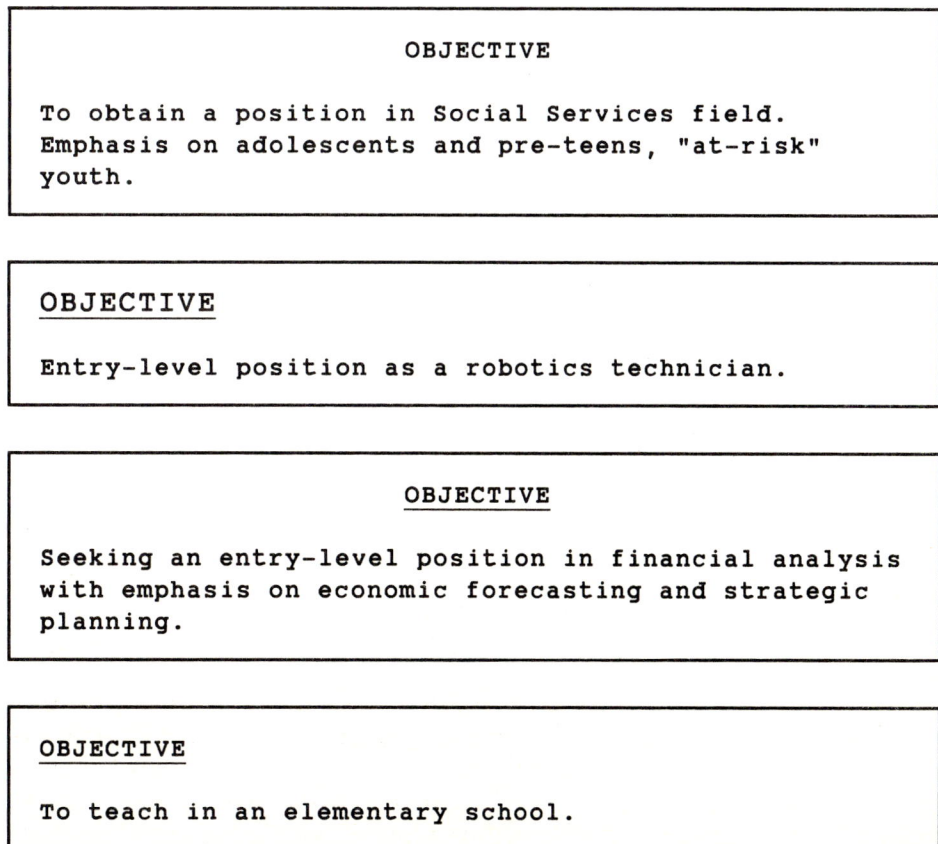

OBJECTIVE

To obtain a position in Social Services field. Emphasis on adolescents and pre-teens, "at-risk" youth.

OBJECTIVE

Entry-level position as a robotics technician.

OBJECTIVE

Seeking an entry-level position in financial analysis with emphasis on economic forecasting and strategic planning.

OBJECTIVE

To teach in an elementary school.

Figure 3-2 Sample occupational objectives.

Stating the skills you want to use is another way to describe your employment objective.

> "Desire position where knowledge of C, FORTRAN, COBOL, RPG II, or BASIC programming can be utilized."

Of course, any of these methods can be combined or modified. What is important is that you get your message across, clearly and concisely, as to the type of work you desire. Once the reader knows who you are and what you want to do, the next items should reflect why you are able to do it.

3.4   LISTING EDUCATIONAL BACKGROUND

Educational entries should include any relevant training received after high school. The only time a high school entry is encouraged is if it would be a highlight (for instance, applying to be an athletic trainer or a food service director for the school district from which you graduated) or if you received specialized training through a Vocational-Technical school and it is related to your occupational objective.

The highest relevant degree or training is listed first with name of institution, city, state, and degree(s) awarded (or whatever accomplishment was attained: granted diploma, earned 45 credits, awarded certificate, etc.) Any highlights of the educational experience, such as grade point averages, honors conferred, special projects or recognitions, should also be included (Fig. 3-3).

```
Westmoreland County Community College
Youngwood, PA
Degree - Associate in Applied Science    May 1990
Major - Computer Science
Q.P.A.: Overall - 3.4    Major - 3.5

Courses:  Assembler, BASIC, COBOL, Fortran, Pascal,
          Database Management, Systems Analysis,
          Calculus, Operations Science

Computer Experience: Vax-11-780, Prime 2250. Have
          also worked with the following PCs: IBM
          PC XT, TRS-80, Apple IIGS, Commodore Amiga,
          Panasonic Exec-Partner

Mon-Valley Vocational-Technical School
Speers, PA
Degree - Received Certificate    June 1987
Major - Data Processing

Courses:  Significant major courses included COBOL,
          Fortran

Honors: Elected Vice-President of VICA (Vocational
          Industrial Clubs of America)
```

Figure 3-3 Education examples.

```
Duquesne University
Pittsburgh, PA
Degree: Master of Science     Dec. 1985
Major:  General Education
Concentration: Counseling/Learning
        Theory/Administration

Computer Experience: Capable with business and
        education software including WordPerfect,
        Lotus 1-2-3, Symphony, Appleworks, and other
        packaged programs

University of Pennsylvania
Philadelphia, PA
Degree: Bachelor of Arts      Aug. 1976
Major: International Relations
Concentration: Eastern European Studies

Courses: Included language study in Russian, Polish,
         and Italian; History, Political Science,
         and culture studies of East Europe;
         International Economics

Projects: Worked as an Assistant Lexicographer/Typist
          for Professor who wrote an English/Serbian
          dictionary
```

Figure 3-3   *(Continued)*

```
General Motors Training Center, Monroeville, PA

Degree:   Obtained Diagnostic Certification  Jan. 1987

Courses:  Diagnostic Certification for automotive
          cranking, charging system, and carburetor
          diagnosis, repair, and adjustment.
```

```
U.S. Army Military Police School, Ft. McClellan, AL

Degree:   Certificate of M.P. Training    March 1986

Courses:  Completed special courses in weaponry,
          unarmed self-defense, laws and regulations
          in law enforcement, hostage rescue
          techniques, and investigations.
```

Figure 3-4   "Other" education examples.

If your program of study contained courses of special value, list them. Do not assume that all readers will know what you have learned if your major was computer science, education, or graphic communications. Tell what equipment you used, in what area you specialized, what languages you studied, and so on. Educational experiences attained through military, continuing education, or other settings are also important entries (see Fig. 3-4).

3.5   HIGHLIGHTING EMPLOYMENT EXPERIENCES

Many people think an outline with job title, employer name, location, and length of service is sufficient for a resume. It is not. Outlines read like obituaries and may give that same impression of applicants.

The employment section of your resume should indicate not only what jobs you have had, but also *how* you have performed in those positions. Emphasize skills used and don't be afraid to acknowledge your contributions to the company.

3.5.1   PAID WORK EXPERIENCE

This category should include information on each job you have held that will be important to the employers who read your resume. Not every job you have ever held since your paper route days should be listed, only the ones that have relevance based on what you want to do and who the reader is.

Some people title this category "Significant Experience" to differentiate relevant and non-related work. THE RESUME WRITER uses the title "Career-Related Experience." Each item should be listed in reverse chronological order and should include your job title, the name of the company, city, state, dates of employment or length of experience, and most importantly, a brief description of your position. To help you condense this "brief description" of your work, THE RESUME WRITER allows you no more than six lines of text—enough for 50–60 words (see Fig. 3-5).

```
CAREER RELATED:

Mineral Fiber Manufacturing Corporation, Coshocton, OH
Position: Chemist     Jan. 1986 - Present
Perform QC of raw materials and of various asphalt
and rubberized products. Consult with outside firms
in manufacturing products to correct specifications.
Plan product improvements and develop new products.
Researched and created a new composite for single
membrane torch-down roofing.

Allied Chemical Corporation, Newell, PA
Position: Chemist (part time summer) June - Aug. 1985
Analyzed emissions for stack gasses at nitric-sulphuric
acid plant and performed routine lab analyses.
```

Figure 3-5 *Examples of paid work experience.*

```
CAREER RELATED:

William F. Doctorson, MD, Putnam, CT
Position: Office Manager   May 1982 - Oct. 1987
Supervised 4 clerical employees; oversaw all billing
procedures, incl. insurance form processing, ICD-9
and CPT coding, accounts receivable, accounts
payable; typed, filed, posted transactions; scheduled
appointments, handled telephone and window reception;
developed billing system for more effective
recordkeeping.

OTHER EXPERIENCE:

Also held a variety of part-time, seasonal, or
temporary positions as waitress, private tutor,
and amusement park worker.
```

Figure 3-5   *(Continued)*

THE RESUME WRITER will list a set of ACTION VERBS if you press the F2 key on the keyboard (see Fig. 3-6). These words will prove useful when you describe your job responsibilities.

Use action verbs (see Fig. 3-7) and specific terms instead of vague descriptions. For example, "Supervised staff of ten people" sounds much better than "Responsible for supervising staff." "Managed budget of $120,000" is preferred to "Duties included managing budget." Remember, you want the reader to get a clear, strong picture of you as a worker. Use strong action words in your descriptions and stress your accomplishments.

Press F2 key to view Action Verbs

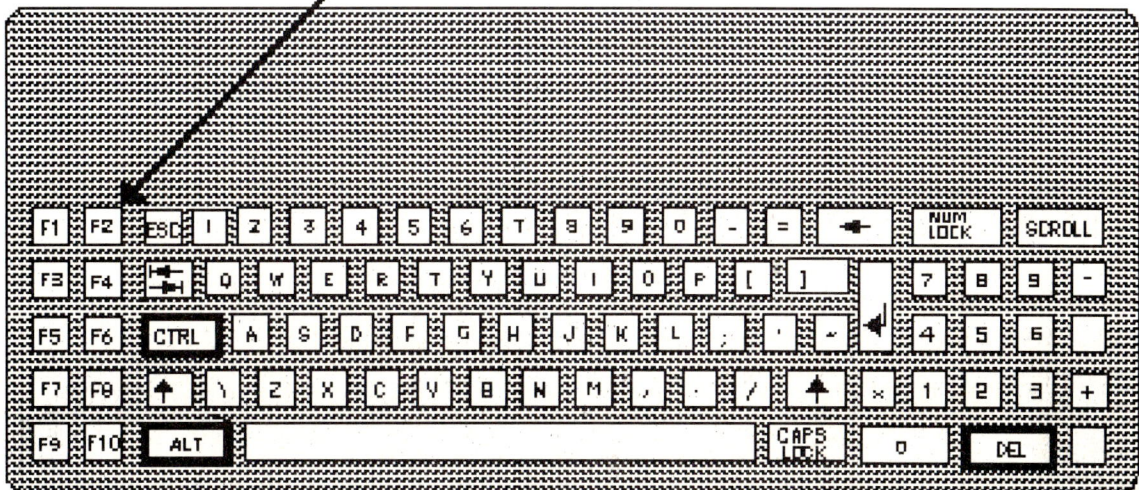

Figure 3-6   PC keyboard with F2 key highlighted.

Action Verbs

Accomplished	Contracted	Filed	Modified	Repaired
Achieved	Controlled	Filtered	Monitored	Replaced
Acted	Coordinated	Figured	Motivated	Reported
Advocated	Corrected	Fixed	Navigated	Represented
Activated	Corresponded	Formulated	Negotiated	Researched
Adapted	Counselled	Forwarded	Observed	Resolved
Adjusted	Created	Founded	Obtained	Responded
Administered	Deferred	Gathered	Operated	Restored
Addressed	Defined	Generated	Ordered	Retrieved
Adopted	Delegated	Governed	Organized	Reviewed
Advertised	Delivered	Guided	Originated	Revised
Advised	Demonstrated	Handled	Oversaw	Revitalized
Aligned	Designed	Headed	Painted	Rewrote
Analyzed	Detailed	Helped	Participated	Saved
Anticipated	Detected	Hired	Perfected	Scheduled
Applied	Determined	Identified	Performed	Screened
Appraised	Developed	Illustrated	Persuaded	Selected
Arbitrated	Devised	Implemented	Photographed	Served
Arranged	Diagnosed	Improved	Piloted	Shaped
Ascertained	Directed	Improvised	Pioneered	Shipped
Assembled	Discovered	Increased	Planned	Simplified
Assessed	Dispensed	Indexed	Predicted	Sketched
Assisted	Displayed	Indoctrinated	Prepared	Sorted
Attained	Disproved	Influenced	Prescribed	Sparked
Audited	Dissected	Informed	Presented	Specified
Arranged	Distributed	Initiated	Preserved	Stimulated
Balanced	Diverted	Innovated	Presided	Straightened
Budgeted	Documented	Inspected	Printed	Streamlined
Built	Drafted	Inspired	Processed	Strengthened
Calculated	Dramatized	Installed	Produced	Studied
Calibrated	Edited	Instituted	Programmed	Supervised
Catalogued	Educated	Instructed	Projected	Supplied
Chaired	Effected	Integrated	Promoted	Surveyed
Changed	Electrified	Interpreted	Proposed	Synthesized
Charted	Eliminated	Interviewed	Protected	Systematized
Classified	Enforced	Introduced	Provided	Tabulated
Coached	Enlarged	Invented	Publicized	Taught
Collaborated	Entertained	Inventoried	Published	Tested
Collected	Established	Investigated	Purchased	Trained
Communicated	Estimated	Judged	Quoted	Transcribed
Compiled	Evaluated	Launched	Raised	Transferred
Completed	Examined	Led	Reasoned	Translated
Composed	Executed	Lectured	Recommended	Transmitted
Computed	Exhibited	Located	Reconciled	Treated
Conceptualized	Expanded	Maintained	Recorded	Tutored
Conciliated	Expedited	Managed	Recruited	Unified
Conducted	Explained	Mapped	Reduced	Upgraded
Confronted	Expressed	Marketed	Referred	Updated
Consolidated	Extracted	Measured	Rehabilitated	Verified
Constructed	Fabricated	Mediated	Related	Vitalized
Conserved	Facilitated	Mentored	Rendered	Worked
Consulted	Familiarized	Modeled	Reorganized	Wrote

Figure 3-7 Action Verbs useful in resume writing.

3.5.2 UNPAID WORK EXPERIENCE

If you are low on actual paid work experience, do not neglect to include internships, cooperative education assignments, volunteer work, or other applicable experience. If you were not paid for a certain job but were responsible for getting the work done, it can be used as an item under employment experience. (It is a good idea to indicate in parentheses if the job falls into one of these "unpaid" categories.) If you have outlined your significant, career-related work history but would like the reader to see other experience you have, you can do this under another category: "Other Experience," and list additional jobs without going into as much detail (Fig. 3-8). THE RESUME WRITER will ask you if you would like to do this.

At this point the reader of your resume has a good idea of who you are, what you want to do for the company, and why you are able to do it. But you should not stop at this point. A good advertiser will continue to supply information that will convince the audience that this product is different from the rest and worthy of testing.

If all commercials and all advertisements looked exactly the same (same promotional pitch, same design, same length, etc.), we wouldn't be able to tell much difference. In fact, it wouldn't matter which product we did try or buy because they would all look the same! If every resume submitted to employers would be identical (same categories, same layout, same length), then they would also become useless marketing tools.

You need to ask yourself "How am I different from the rest of the competition? What else have I done, do I know, can I do, that I want employers to know about?" With the addition of this significant information, your resume can become the creative marketing tool it is meant to be. You have the foundation; now continue building.

```
USX Corporation, Pittsburgh, PA

Position: Computer Science Intern  May 1988 - Dec. 1988

Worked in Headquarters Systems Development
Department. Performed COBOL programming on IBM
mainframe. Attended introductory courses in LOTUS
1-2-3 and DBase III, learning DBASE programming and
NATURAL programming using ADABAS data base system.
```

```
Kids Country Daycare, Geistown, PA

Position: Coordinator (Volunteer) May 1989 - present

Plan activities, record progress, and schedule events
for ten four- to five-year-olds.
```

Figure 3-8 Examples of unpaid work experience.

chapter 4

Additional Categories
of Information

LEARNING OBJECTIVES:

Chapter Four introduces other category entries you may wish to include on your resume. You will learn about creating categories for:

- Skills and competencies
- Military experiences
- Activities, hobbies, and interests
- Professional memberships and associations
- Publications and other accomplishments
- Honors and community/civic activities
- What else needs to be conveyed?
- Personal statements or summaries

4.1 SKILLS AND COMPETENCIES

In some instances, job applicants may possess work skills or aptitudes which are not readily evident from reading previous entries. Candidates, for example, with a computer science degree but with no real world experience, may want the resume screener to know the variety of programming languages they have mastered and types of hardware and software they have used.

Some applicants for accounting or finance positions may have developed clerical skills as a result of part-time or seasonal work. While typing, filing, or ten-key calculator skills are not necessarily posted as requirements for every entry-level accounting job, possessing these skills may make the difference as to which candidate an employer will call for an interview.

Aptitudes, or skills rooted in your abilities, are also known as "transferable skills." Transferable skills move with you throughout your working career. While work skills are tied to job titles, transferable skills are related to innate or developed abilities. These talents may have resulted from work experiences, but may also have developed from hobbies, volunteer positions, or interests you have.

Speaking in front of an audience (public-speaking/presentation skills), persuading people to buy products (sales), or calming an irate customer (customer service), are all examples of situations where transferable skills are developed. If your background has provided you with such experience, you may want to highlight this ability with a separate category entry on your resume.

Also known as qualification summaries, skill or competency categories may be entered as a paragraph or as a list.

```
                    Qualifications


A computer programmer . . . Experienced in a
manufacturing environment . . . Proven skill in
trouble-shooting to maintain systems and reduce down
time . . . Developed effective, practical solutions
that increase productivity . . . Manufacturing
exposure includes machining and turning centers,
FANUC 6T, FANUC 6M, GE 1050, and OKUMA controls.
```

Figure 4-1 A sample qualifications entry.

```
              Programming and operations skills

HARDWARE . . .   DEC VAX, Data General.
OPERATING
  SYSTEMS . . .  VAX/VMS, MDSI-150.
LANGUAGES . . .  ForTran, BASIC, COMPACT II, APT,
                 Auto-Trol, Series 7000 CAD/CAM
```

Figure 4-2 A sample skills entry.

4.2 MILITARY EXPERIENCE

Many candidates with military history will choose to include it with employment or experience entries. If you are an applicant for jobs where a good military record will be an asset (jobs in the Defense sector, government intelligence, and so on), list your military experience separately.

```
                          MILITARY

    U.S. Army

    Rank:  Specialist 4    1980-82

    Served as a clerk in the Headquarters, V Corps Support
    Command. Handled normal typing of orders and letters,
    prepared charts for seminars and conferences. Carried
    classified materials and maintained an orderly flow of
    paperwork through the office. Awarded the Army
    Commendation (a rarity for a two-year draftee).
```

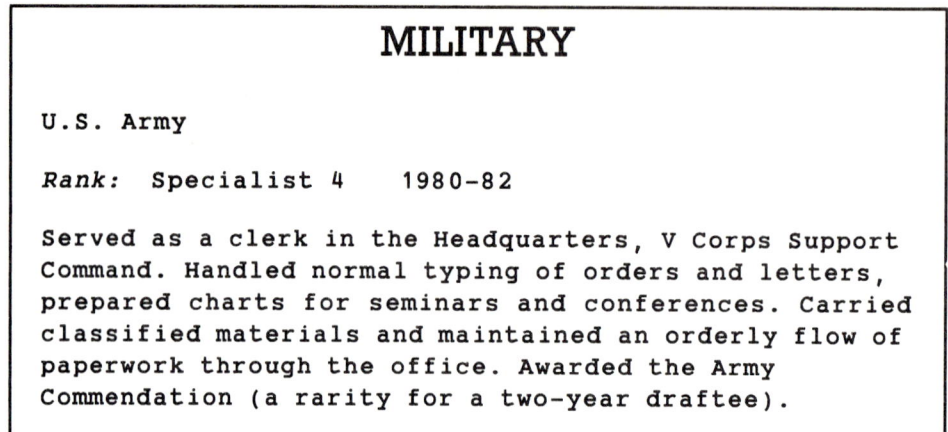

Figure 4-3 A military experience illustration.

4.3 ACTIVITIES, HOBBIES, AND INTERESTS

Categories for activities, hobbies, or interests may be added if you think this information is relevant to the position you are seeking. Organized sports shows a team player; cross-stitch indicates a person who can work with fine detail; chess reflects an analytical thinker.

Think about what you want to do and where you want to do it—that is the key to including this type of information. If a connection exists between your activity, hobby, or interest, include it. If not, it is considered "fluff" and will only take up space on your resume.

4.4 PROFESSIONAL MEMBERSHIPS AND ASSOCIATIONS

Affiliations with "professional" organizations is an important inclusion for your resume. The fact that you belong to such groups shows a recruiter you are interested in advancing your career.

Your resume is intended to "showcase" your professional skills and accomplishments. Social, political, religious, or otherwise controversial areas are best omitted unless involvement within the organization points to a directly related skill. Aspiring financial planners, for instance, should include membership in the local Rotary Club or Business and Professional Women's Club since it indicates a source of potential clients.

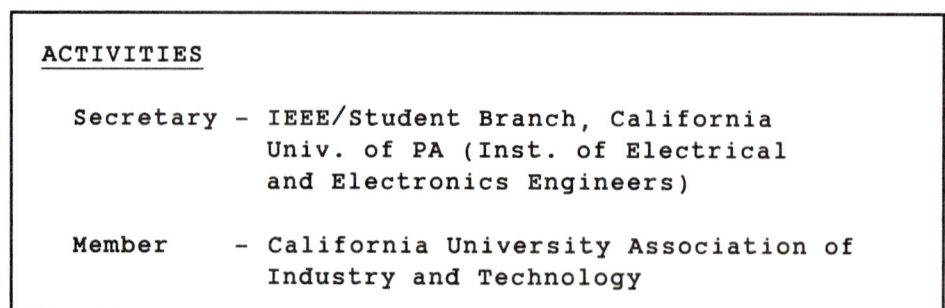

```
    ACTIVITIES

      Secretary - IEEE/Student Branch, California
                  Univ. of PA (Inst. of Electrical
                  and Electronics Engineers)

      Member    - California University Association of
                  Industry and Technology
```

Figure 4-4 Student membership in professional organizations.

4.5 PUBLICATIONS AND OTHER ACCOMPLISHMENTS

If you have written articles, conducted research, received a patent, or have some other kind of accomplishment, set it apart from other information on your resume. Accomplishments of this kind label you as an achiever.

If you do have such accomplishments to include in your resume use the combination format offered by THE RESUME WRITER, as explained in Chapter 5.

4.6 HONORS AND COMMUNITY/CIVIC ACTIVITIES

While academic honors appear under education categories, recognition you have received in other instances is listed separately. Recognition as top salesperson, appointments to boards or advisory committees, and honors bestowed for civic leadership or volunteerism are admirable testaments to your work ethic and values.

In THE RESUME WRITER you will find a section titled "Honors" for this type of information.

4.7 WHAT ELSE NEEDS TO BE CONVEYED?

Each person is a unique individual with a highly diverse background. In considering the information you wish to include in your resume, the categories presented thus far may not be inclusive. These are suggestions only, so be inventive.

You know *you* better than anyone else. Do you need to add an entry for certification or licensure? seminars attended? computer literacy? career highlights? strengths? other facts? No two resumes should ever look alike since no two job seekers are the same. Construct the categories to fit your background; don't try to squeeze your background into someone else's categories. Explore the Combination resume format explained in the next chapter. Using THE RESUME WRITER, this format will allow you more scope for expression of a personal statement than the traditional Chronological format.

4.8 PERSONAL STATEMENTS OR SUMMARIES

There may be times when some facts that you want to include won't fit neatly into a similar category. A statement at the end of your resume (personal statement, summary, or additional facts) written in list or paragraph form can tie these pieces together. A willingness to travel or relocate, additional characteristics related to work, health, or other personal data, opinions, and so on, might be information important to your personal commercial.

Keep in mind the message you have been reading all along—only include information if it supports your candidacy for a position. Personal statements that prove you have "the right stuff" will give a powerful ending to your resume; statements that simply add unrelated detail will dilute your presentation.

The key to all resume entries, always, is to include only positive information that is relevant to the type of position you are seeking. Use information only if it demonstrates that you possess professional skills and that you know how to use them.

Now that you have assembled all the raw material, you must decide how to arrange these details on paper. Read on to learn about selecting a format and a layout style for your resume.

chapter 5

Choosing Formats
and Layouts

LEARNING OBJECTIVES:

By reading this section, you will review specific formats and layout styles for presenting your credentials in a resume:

- Essential formats
  - Chronological
  - Functional
  - Combination
- Essential layouts
  - The basic layout
  - The traditional layout
  - Other designs
- Special resumes for special people
- More sample Formats and Styles

5.1 ESSENTIAL FORMATS

You can find as many resume formats as flavors of ice cream. With a careful review, however, you will see that most of them are merely adaptations of one of three very standard formats: chronological, functional, or something called the combination format. Read the following sections on formats and study the sample resumes in Section 5.4.

5.1.1 CHRONOLOGICAL FORMATS

The chronological resume (Fig. 5-1) is the most commonly known and most widely used format. Experience and education are listed in reverse chronological order, that is, the most recent job or training appears first. The reasoning behind this is simple—your most recent past (usually the last two to three years) is what gets the attention of employers. It reveals what has been important in your recent work or educational experience.

The chronological format may not be suitable for candidates with little or no on-the-job experience. In those cases it would highlight the obvious fact that experience is missing. These individuals would therefore do well to consider using the functional format for their resume.

Chronological formats are suitable for showing growth in a particular career field for those candidates that have a base of experience in that field. The chronology should directly relate to the position you are seeking. It is not necessary to list jobs all the way back to your first lemonade stand, unless those experiences are highlights.

If there is a drawback to the chronological resume, it is that this format emphasizes time, instead of achievement. Working somewhere for two and a half years is not what's important—it's what contributions you made in that time that count.

Use a chronological format when your most recent work relates to the position you want, and when you will not need to include other entries to demonstrate work skills.

5.1.2 FUNCTIONAL FORMATS

Applicants who have a history of unrelated work experiences, who are very limited in work experience, or who are changing careers, may elect to utilize a "skills" or functional resume (Fig. 5-2). This format rejects a chronology of employment and education and focuses on groupings of skills and competencies.

The grouping of skills into categories will depend on the applicant's particular occupational objective. The headings could directly represent work-related skills, such as "Administrative" or "Sales/Marketing." Or they could represent transferable skills such as "Customer Service" or "Analytic Ability." Even aptitudes rooted in personality are acceptable—"Motivational," "Detail Oriented." References to where and when these skills were developed are not stressed.

One of the problems in using a functional resume is that it is easy for job-hoppers to disguise a poor employment record with this format and can make relatively inexperienced workers sound overly impressive. The addition of organization names and length of employment can lend credibility to a functional resume.

Use a functional format if you want to focus on skills rather than credentials. If you have had unrelated employment experiences or have had limited experience, are changing careers, or are re-entering the work environment after an absence, this format will serve your personal commercial best.

Because of the more personalized, less itemized, nature of the functional resume, THE RESUME WRITER simply prompts you for one section title after another until you are done. For each section you may write up to six lines of freeform* text to briefly describe your attributes as they relate to the subject matter of the section.

---

*Freeform, as its name implies, means you can layout the text in this section whichever way you like, as you would were you to use a word processor.

PENNY ANN JOHNS
2020 Prospect Lane
Bradenville, PA 15620
(412) 539-9999

OBJECTIVE

To obtain an entry level position as an accountant with possible advancement opportunities within the company.

EDUCATION

University of Pittsburgh at Johnstown, Johnstown, PA
Degree: Bachelor of Arts   April 1991
Major: Business   *Minor:* Computer Science
Concentration: Accounting
Q.P.A.:   Overall - 3.24 Major: - 3.34

Courses: Principles of Financial Accounting I &
               II, Business Calculus, Communications,
               Intro to BASIC, Exploring Computers,
               Economics, Management, Corporate
               Finance, Advanced Accounting I & II,
               Cost Accounting.

Languages: BASIC, Fortran, COBOL, Pascal

The Boyd School, Pittsburgh, PA
Degree: Certificate   June 1988
Major: Business
Concentration: Computerized Office Administration
Q.P.A.:   Overall - 3.50

Courses: Word Processing, Computerized Office
               Administration, Data Processing, BASIC
               Programming, Lotus 1-2-3, Accounting,
               IBM PC, Business Communications

WORK EXPERIENCE

Giant Eagle, Johnstown, PA
Position: Cashier   June 1988 - Present
Continuous interaction with customers and exchange of money; take on all responsibilities and operations of cash registers and video/lottery department.

Pittsburgh Marathon, Pittsburgh, PA
Position: Data Processor   Feb. 1988 - May 1988
Processed data vital to the operation of the marathon.

REFERENCES

Available upon request

Figure 5-1   Chronological resume with basic layout.

```
                        CALVIN N. PITTMAN
                        146 Ginger Avenue
                       Johnstown, PA 15904
                          814-266-9999


                            Objective

              Sales Management or Sales Representation


                              Sales

Account manager for direct sales of cellular
phones, telephone systems, facsimile machines, pagers. Developed and
generated sales of up to $5000 within first month of employment.
Worked 50 hours per week for 100% commission. Adept with vendor/
manufacturer representation. Experienced in all aspects of client
contacts set by initial cold calls.


                            Management

Supervised up to 20 people in sales, customer service, and marketing
departments. Assisted in hiring, training, motivating, and evaluating
staff. Planned effective marketing strategy.


                            Computer

Assisted with implementation of, and transition to, computerized
system in sales department. Realized savings of 20% in operating
budgets.


                            Education

California University of Pennsylvania, California, PA Aug. 86
Awarded Bachelor of Science degree - Business Administration
Q.P.A. - 3.6                                     Dean's List Student

TIME:TEXT Priority Management Systems, Pittsburgh, PA Oct. 86
Completed intensive six-hour training seminar for developing effective
organization and planning

                         Work Experience

Performance Cellular, Pittsburgh, PA - Sept. 86 - Oct. 89
Shearson Lehman Hutton, Inc., Pittsburgh, PA - Summer 86
Precision Industries, Washington, PA - Dec. 89 to Present
References Available Upon Request
```

Figure 5-2 Functional resume with traditional layout.

This freedom can be problematic because you need good writing skills to represent yourself well. For this reason it is all the more important that you consult with career services personnel to ensure that your functional resume will do the best possible job of representing you in the job market.

5.1.3 COMBINATION RESUMES

When neither of the above resumes presents the best features of an applicant, altering or combining formats can create one that is more suitable. A combination resume (see Fig. 5-3) is the name of the style which allows selection of the most appropriate parts of the chronological and the functional formats. In addition to personal information and an occupational objective, this format includes a career summary section, a functional skills entry, a chronology of employment, and an educational background section.

The career summary statement incorporates achievements and personal characteristics; the skills section highlights abilities without mention of when and where these skills were obtained; and the chronological histories of employment and education evidence the achievements and skills by presenting company and school names, dates, job titles, duties, and degrees earned. The combination resume is becoming the format of choice because it addresses the presentation of skills *and* allays fears that the job seeker is hiding a weak employment record.

If you are targeting specific opportunities, use the combination resume format. It allows you to tailor your commercial to fit the requirements of each position. Skillful combining of the chronological and functional styles can provide a powerful resume format.

5.2 ESSENTIAL LAYOUTS

Choosing a layout means designing how the information will appear on the paper. Many of the guidelines which apply to graphic arts design will also apply to designing resumes. All readers of resumes want them to be easy to read. Using margins, underlining or bolding important information or headings, and utilizing white space will aid readers as they scan the resume.

A minimum of one inch should be used as a margin on all sides. Good use of white space (also known as empty space) frees the eyes from travelling back and forth, from left to right, all the way down the page.

<u>CAPS AND UNDERLINING</u>, ALL CAPS, **Bolding**, or <u>UPPER and lower case with underlining</u> will make information stand out on the page. If your printer has the capability, you may also want to experiment with Enlarged characters.

There are several layouts which are commonly used in resume design. These should be reviewed and considered, but keep in mind that the ultimate design should be one that supports your choice of format and one that leads the reader effortlessly to the highlights of your resume.

5.2.1 THE BASIC LAYOUT

The basic layout contains a centered personal contact section, and places other section headings at the left margin. Entry items for each section follow another margin roughly halfway between the left margin and the center of the page (see Fig. 5-1).

PENNY JOHNS
2020 Prospect Lane
Bradenville, PA 15620
412-539-9999

OBJECTIVE

A position in a theatre group dealing with public
relations, promotion, and production.

SUMMARY OF QUALITIES

Possess over 25 years experience in performing arts.
Strong communication background. Detail-oriented
and a "follow through" individual. Business education
complements theatre experience.

PUBLIC RELATIONS/PROMOTIONS

Designed numerous newsletters for organizations.
Wrote weekly column for area newspaper dealing
with upcoming performing arts events. Arranged
media coverage of all company performances. Acted
as office manager of an income tax business for
twelve years. Handled all client contact. Developed
forms and organized files.

PERFORMANCE SKILLS

Experienced in speaking, choral, and dancing roles in
a variety of local productions. Also teach cello on a
weekly basis for seven students. Schedule and conduct
rehearsals for area choir.

EDUCATION

University of Pittsburgh, Johnstown, PA
Major: Business   June 1992
Q.P.A.: Overall - 4.00

Courses: Include Computer Science, marketing, sales
          classes.

Pennsylvania State University, University Park, PA
Major: Merchandising   Nov. 1974
Concentration: Clothing construction and retailing
Q.P.A.: Overall - 3.45

Honors: Graduated Cum Laude
        Omicron Nu

Figure 5-3 Combination resume with traditional layout.

PENNY JOHNS   Page 2
2020 Prospect Lane
Bradenville, PA 15620
412-539-9999

                    WORK EXPERIENCE

CAREER RELATED:

Penn Wood Players, Johnstown, PA
Position: Advertising/PR   Jan. 1980 - Dec. 1989
Sold advertising packages to businesses. Brought in over
$10,000 in ads in one three month period. Handled company
public relations. Also worked costuming on occasion.

OTHER EXPERIENCE:

Have also held positions as office secretary, office
manager, pricing clerk, salesclerk and instructor for
area and own businesses.

                      ACTIVITIES

Music performance and appreciation, theatre arts,
traveling, needlework, calligraphy.

                      REFERENCES

              Available upon request

Figure 5-3b Combination resume with traditional layout.

5.2.2 THE TRADITIONAL LAYOUT

The traditional layout also places the personal section in the center. Section headings are centered, and section entries are aligned to the left margin (see Fig. 5-2 and Fig. 5-3). This is the default layout for THE RESUME WRITER, which means that this will be what the system will implement if you don't choose any particular layout of your own.

5.2.3 OTHER DESIGNS

Other layout designs are possible by combining or altering the above examples. Some candidates use a left margin for all entries; some choose to put dates at the left or right margin; others separate section headings from content by using a solid vertical line.

Review the layout designs presented, and then experiment. Find the style that best suits your format and your content. As explained in Chapter Twelve, Section 12.3, THE RESUME WRITER gives you plenty of flexibility in this regard.

5.3 SPECIAL RESUMES FOR SPECIAL PEOPLE

Occasionally, conservative formats and layouts will simply not perform well for special job seekers. Individuals seeking careers in design, photography, commercial art, or advertising may wish to demonstrate creative ability in their resumes. In fact, submitting a conservative resume for positions in these fields may be suicide! For these people, special creative resumes may be the vehicle to show imagination, as well as to market their talent.

A useful alternative for such special individuals would be to use THE RESUME WRITER to collect the raw data for your resume. Then select the Power User[*] option of **Printing To Disk** (Chapter 13). This will allow you to transfer the resume file to, say, an Apple Macintosh or IBM PC desktop publishing system, where, if you know what you are doing, you will find the tools to give full vent to your creative talents.

When choosing a format and layout, consider that your resume should reflect abilities and qualifications. Let it speak for itself.

5.4 MORE SAMPLE FORMATS AND STYLES

For ideas on how you might put together your resume it is always useful to study what has worked for other people, just as a good writer reads the work of other writers, or an artist studies the creations of other artists. What follows is a selection of effective resumes. Study them, take ideas from them, before setting out to create your own personalized document.

---

[*]You, the reader, may qualify as a "Power User" if you are comfortable using a word processor of your choice, and have some familiarity with MS-DOS or PC-DOS on the IBM PC or compatible computer. Chapter 13 explains some of the options open to the Power User.

Calvin N. Pittman

Home Address: Present Address:
146 Ginger Avenue   999 Sunshine Avenue
Johnstown, PA 15904   Johnstown, PA 15904
(412) 266-9999   (412) 539-9999

OBJECTIVE

To secure an entry level professional position in
mechanical engineering or applied physics

EDUCATION

University of Pittsburgh at Johnstown, Johnstown, PA
Degree: Bachelor of Science   April 1990
Major: Mechanical Engineering
Q.P.A.:   Overall - 3.57   Major: - 3.63

Courses: Calculus, Chemistry, Communications,
             Computer Programming, Drafting,
             Dynamics, Physics, Statics, Statistics,
             Strength of Materials, Surveying.

Honors: Dean's List student
             Chi Gamma Psi - Honorary Science and Math
             Fraternity

Software: Fortran, BASIC, AUTOCAD, C, PLOT 10,
             Assembler, RASP

Hardware: VAX, Apple IIc, DEC Rainbow, AT&T 6300

Projects: Designed an external noise reduction
             device for an industrial envelope making
             machine.

WORK EXPERIENCE
CAREER RELATED:
Owens Corning Fiberglass, Huntingdon, PA
Position: Project Engineer Trainee May 1989 -
Sept. 1989
Designed plant equipment and supervised expansion
of production facilities.

OTHER EXPERIENCE:
Foster Construction, Pittsburgh, PA
Position: Carpenter   May 1988 - Aug. 1988
Built pre-fabricated decks, including
understructures.

ACTIVITIES
American Society of Mechanical Engineers, Physics
Tutor, UPJ Ski Team, Darkhorse Intramural Club

Figure 5-4 Chronological resume basic style.

PENNY ANN JOHNS
2020 Prospect Lane
Bradenville, PA 15620
(412) 539-9999

OBJECTIVE
To obtain an entry level position as an accountant with possible advancement opportunities within the company.

EDUCATION
Lorain County Community College, Elyria, OH
Degree: Associate in Science
Major: Computer Science

Courses: Have completed 45 credits in program.
             Expected graduation date is May 1992.
             Courses include: Programming Logic,
             Microcomputer Software Applications,
             Database Design, Database Management.

Languages: BASIC,
             COBOL,
             Assembler

Hardware: Skilled in use of various personal
             computers including IBM PC and
             compatibles, Apple, and other popular
             systems.

Projects: Designed a computerized candidate/job match
             program for college's placement center as
             part of semester project. Program has been
             adopted for use by office.

WORK EXPERIENCE
Lorain County Community College, Elyria, OH
Position: Student Tutor   Jan. 1990 - Present
Provide tutoring to enrolled students in areas of
business math and computer science. Handle up to 12
students per week in both group sessions and
individual tutoring.

McDonald's Restaurant, Cleveland, OH
Position: Crew person   March 1988 - Present
Worked as part of fast food crew in busy downtown
location. Worked full-time until college classes
began. Now employed for 20 hours each week.

ACTIVITIES
College Computer Club (President 1991)
Active in community emergency medical services council
Enjoy softball, aerobic dance, and chess

Figure 5-5 Chronological resume traditional style.

Calvin N. Pittman
146 Ginger Avenue
Johnstown, PA 15904
(412) 266-9999

OBJECTIVE
Position as an Environmental Technician.

EDUCATION
California University of Pennsylvania, California, PA
Degree: Bachelor of Science   Dec. 1991
Major: Environmental Technology
Concentration: Water Analysis
Q.P.A.:   Overall – 2.90 Major – 3.10
Courses: Biostatistical Analysis, Soil Science,
                   Water Treatment Facilities, Biotic
                   Indicators of Water Quality, Biological
                   Research Investigation, Analytical and
                   Organic Chemistry, Techniques of Water
                   and Waste Water Analysis.

Honors: Dean's List
                   Beta Beta Beta – National Honorary
                   Science Fraternity

Projects: Research project: "Spawning Site
                   Selection in Cichlasoma Nigrofasciatum"
                   Delivered address to the Pennsylvania
                   Academy of Science on research topic.

Rensselaer Polytechnic Institute, Troy, NY
Degree: Master of Science
Major: Environmental Engineering

Courses: Currently completing program in
                   environmental engineering and
                   environmental sciences.
                   Q.P.A. to-date – 3.9
                   Anticipated graduation – December 1992

Projects: Thesis research is in the area of solid
                   and hazardous waste disposal and
                   resource-recovery systems

WORK EXPERIENCE
EMS Landscaping, Penn Hills, PA
Position: Landscaper (summer job)   1985 – 1987
Performed general landscaping for natural gas
companies. Gained significant mechanical experience,
read maps, repaired equipment, and organized daily
routes. Earned funds to pay all summer expenses
and contribute to college tuition costs.

Figure 5-6 Two page chronological resume (page 1).

Calvin N. Pittman   Page 2

ACTIVITIES
  University Student Government Representative, member
  of Student Cabinet (California University)
  Graduate Student Council (Rensselaer Institute)
  Interests include: Trout fishing, breeding and
  raising tropical fish, skiing.

REFERENCES
  Available upon request

Figure 5-6   Two page chronological resume (page 2).

CALVIN N. PITTMAN
2345 Crystal Apartments
Cherry Hill, NJ 08034
609-427-9999

Objective
To provide professional gerontology services.
Long term goal is to achieve position of Facilities
Administrator.

Qualifications
Earned a Bachelor degree in gerontology and an
Associate Degree in therapeutic recreation.
Experienced in program development, publicity,
and service delivery.

Planning and Coordination
As program assistant for senior citizen center,
planned and implemented weekly activities and
exercises for a two-year period. Organized and
supervised outings. Handled publicity for nutrition
and homebound meals programs. Coordinated an Open
House for the community. Created "Seniorcise 90," a
low-impact, low-intensity exercise competition.

Therapeutic Training and Competencies
As part of a year-long internship, conducted a
support group for recent widows and widowers
using reminiscence therapy, guided imagery, and
socialization. Handled small caseload of residents
at a personal care home where sensory training and
reality orientation were utilized.

Administration
Developed and submitted a grant proposal which
was selected for funding and resulted in an award
of $25,000 to the senior center.

Interests and Involvement
Engage in, and can teach, wood carving,
ballroom dancing, and exercise. As volunteer
for intergenerational visitation program, visit
homebound elderly on a weekly basis.

References
Professional and personal references available upon
request.

Figure 5-7 *Functional resume layout one.*

PENNY ANN JOHNS
2020 Prospect Lane
Bradenville, PA 15620
412-593-9999

OBJECTIVE
Position as manager-trainee in the retail apparel
industry

SUMMARY OF QUALIFICATIONS
Include supervisory skills and seven years experience
in sales. Motivated individual who excelled in
management and business courses.

SALES
As Avon representative and beauty consultant,
developed territory and solid client base. Realize at
least 18% sales increase each year. Hire, train, and
supervise new reps (up to 20 per year). Won campaign
sales award four times and named top salesperson in
region for 1990.

FASHION AWARENESS
After college, spent summer semester abroad studying
and travelling in Europe. Gained considerable
understanding of various fashion influences.

EDUCATIONAL BACKGROUND
Awarded Associate Degree in Business from Essex
Community College in Baltimore, MD. Earned 12 credits
in accounting, 9 credits in communications, 9 credits
in psychology, and 30 credits in management.

PERSONAL DATA
Willing to travel and relocate . . . Excellent
appearance, grooming, and health . . . Student in
continuing education computer and human resource
management classes . . . Avid reader of fashion
periodicals

ADDITIONAL INFORMATION
References, transcripts, or other information will be
provided upon request.

Figure 5-8 Functional resume layout two.

PENNY ANN JOHNS
308 Stephenson Circle
Clearwater, FL 34615
813-447-9999

Objective
Administrative assistant/office manager

Qualifications Summary
Offering skills in data entry, computer operations,
project coordination, scheduling, and staff training.

Office Skills
Data entry and typing at 65 wpm. Skilled in use of
a variety of business software packages including
WordPerfect 5.0, FirstChoice, Symphony, dBase III and
Alpha IV. Ten-key calculator and photocopier skills.
Some programming ability in BASIC and C languages.

Communications/Coordination
Design and produce company monthly newsletter.
Train new staff in correct office procedures
including client reception. Work with service
providers to organize projects involving "800"
and "900" telephone services. Handle arrangements
and represent company at national trade shows.

Significant Accomplishments
Designed and implemented new automated filing system
for greater efficiency. Wrote and produced office
procedure manual to simplify day-to-day operations.

Education
Pinellas Vocational Technical Institute, Clearwater, FL
Awarded Certificate in Computer Operations - 1989

Employment
Precision Software, Inc., Clearwater, FL
Senior Account Manager - January 1989 to present

Home Shopping Network, Inc., Clearwater, FL
Order Taker - June 1986 to December 1988

Figure 5-9 Functional resume layout three.

Calvin N. Pittman
231 Dandy Blvd
Honolulu, HI 96822
808-954-9999

Objective
A position as an elementary teacher or other occupation
where I may utilize my academic training with young
people.

Significant Experience
Taught 22 second grade students and 18 fourth grade
students as part of student teaching assignments.
Planned, instructed, and evaluated daily course of
study. Lectured and demonstrated with individual
learning centers and audio-visual teaching aids.
Experienced with mainstreamed learning disabled
children.

Other Teaching
Taught summer vacation bible school for five years,
grades one to four. Spent one summer as teacher's
aide for pre-schoolers enrolled in church school.

Accomplishments
+ Won award as most innovative educator in college
  program
+ Was complimented by student teaching supervisor
  for being able to develop self-expression in
  students.

Other Experience
Helped finance college costs by working part-time for
travel industry company as local tour guide.

Miscellaneous
Have completed courses in teaching English as a second
language. Hobbies and interests include horseback
riding, personal computing, and cross-cultural
studies. Certified in CPR and basic first aid.

Education
University of Hawaii at Manoa, Honolulu, HI
Degree: Bachelor of Science   May 1991
Major: Education
Concentration: Elementary
QPA: Overall - 3.5   Major - 3.75

Certifications: Instructional Level I (HI)

Figure 5-10 Combination resume style one.

CALVIN N. PYTMUSZ
123 NOBILE ROAD, APT. 23
CHICAGO, IL 60626
312-973-9999 (home)
312-973-8888 (messages)

Objective

To teach in a Community or Junior College. Areas of interest include computer science, mathematics, or electronics technology.

Educational Background

Master of Science / Education-Vocational and Technical
Education
University of Illinois
Urbana, IL
August 1991   QPA. 4.0

Master of Science / Electrical Engineering

Technical University of Warsaw
Warsaw, Poland
November 1984   Honors graduate

Experience

Community College of Allegheny County, Pittsburgh, PA

Taught computer science courses at the beginner and intermediate levels. Involved in advisement of cooperative education students.   August 1988-May 1990

Factory of Electrical Lamps, Warsaw, Poland

Planned and supervised renovation of electrical facilities for 24 hour energy supply. Coordinated operations of 20 member energy maintenance team.
July 1986-May 1988

High School No 21, Minsk, Poland

Taught mathematics to high school students. September 1985-May 1986

Research Assistant, Technical University of Warsaw/
Physics Institute, Warsaw, Poland

As part of graduate coursework, conducted experiments on the photoelectric effects in semiconductors.

Figure 5-11 Combination resume power user option (page 1).

Pytmusz, Calvin N.   page 2

Professional Memberships
Illinois Society of Electrical Engineers

Computer Languages
Fluent in BASIC, C, COBOL, Fortran, and Pascal

Foreign Languages
Fluency in Polish, Russian, and German.

Community Involvement
Volunteer for Mayor's task force on the homeless.
Serve one day each month at local shelter.

Personal
Married, two children. Enjoy classical music, soccer,
desktop publishing. Vacation time spent in experiencing
different states across country (have visited 31 to
date).

References, transcripts,
publication list,
and courses taught
available upon request

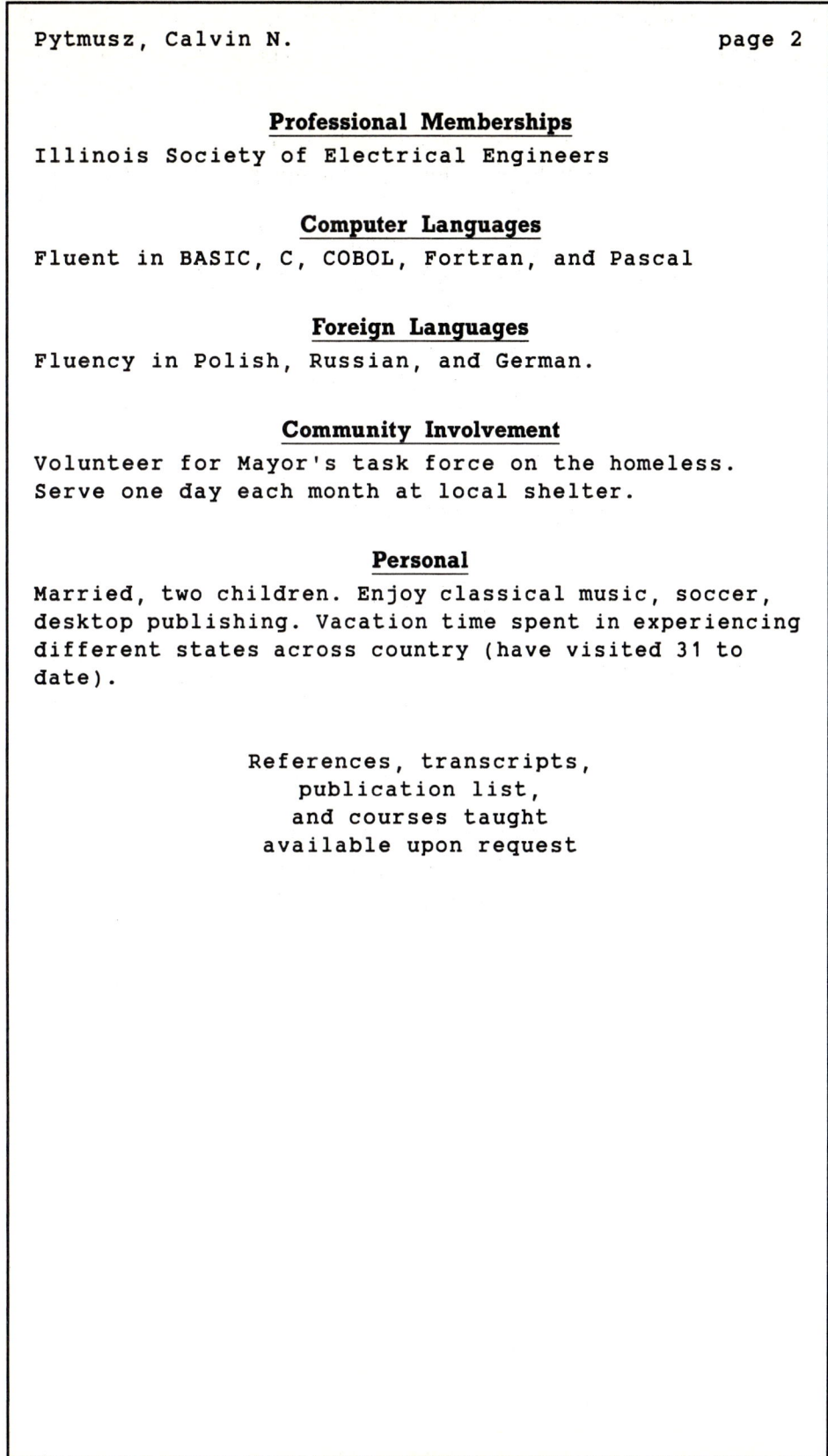

Figure 5-11b Combination resume power user option (page 2).

PENNY   JOHNS
2020 High Street, Englewood, CO 80110   (303)-999-9999

O B J E C T I V E:
An opportunity to serve as a company's relocation consultant

CONSULTING EXPERIENCE
<> Owner/operator of private consulting firm; currently over 325 individual and organizational clients. Consult in areas of image, career development, relocation.
<> Created and conducted seminar on "how to make your first move" for recent college graduates. Presented topic over 200 times in past two years on 116 college campuses.
<> Have worked extensively to provide programming for community agencies such as chambers of commerce, YMCAs, educational institutions, community health centers, and so on.

REAL ESTATE EXPERIENCE
<> Licensed (PA) sales representative. Worked directly with variety of clients to secure listings, show properties, negotiate offers, & refer to appropriate lenders.
<> Prepared advertisements and copy for media.
<> Consistently surpassed sales quotas.

ADDITIONAL SKILLS
<> Created and published brochure for house and apartment hunters.
<> Served as a volunteer mediator for community, resolving landscaping disputes between property owners.
<> Member, National Speakers Association.
<> As part of a two-career professional marriage, have coordinated relocation of own family four times.
<> **Willing to travel or relocate!**

Employment:

Penny For Your Thoughts - Englewood, CO
Position: Owner (self-employed)   1985-present

Three V's Real Estate - Monessen, PA
Position: Sales representative   1983-1985

Education:

Howard University, Washington, D.C.
BA, Economics   1980

Figure 5-12 Individualized layout (power user option).

chapter 6

Finishing Touches

LEARNING OBJECTIVES:

This chapter presents a checklist of items to consider before you create the final product—your completed resume:

- ▫ Image is everything
  - ▫ Editing
  - ▫ Proofreading
  - ▫ Choosing paper
  - ▫ Additional tips and reminders

6.1 IMAGE IS EVERYTHING

A resume equates to a personal sales pitch. All your talent, experience, and hard work will get you nowhere if you present it in writing in an unprofessional manner. Unfortunately, many resumes land up in the "circular file" or the "funny folder" before employers have had a chance to finish reading them. Typos, grammatical errors, spelling mistakes, typeovers, and other "goofs" will certainly spoil your message. Employers will have made up their minds about you without you ever having a chance to say a word. Your resume speaks about and for you—be certain it conveys a polished, competent image.

6.1.1 EDITING

When you first use THE RESUME WRITER, you will be presented with a prompt on the very first screen (Fig. 6-1). The prompt asks you if you have a

```
                    THE RESUME WRITER
                       Version 1.0

                          by
            Paul Layne & Bernard John Poole
          University of Pittsburgh at Johnstown

          Copyright © 1991, all rights reserved


          Do you have a rough draft of your resume (Y/N)?
```

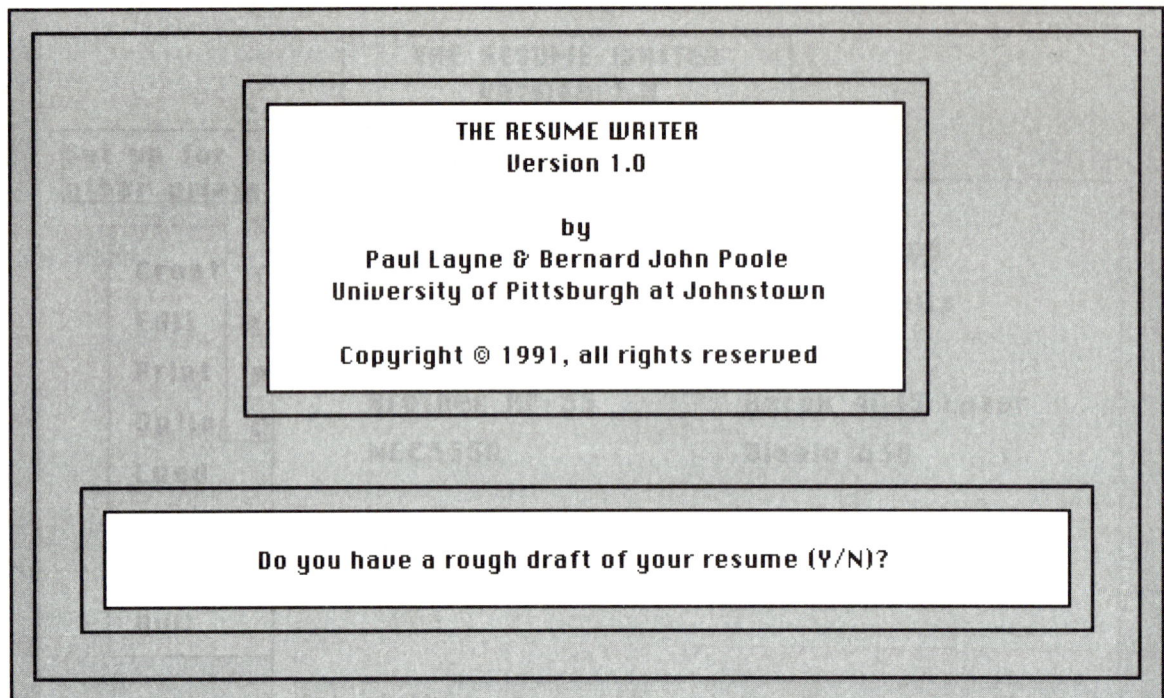

Figure 6-1   Introductory screen for THE RESUME WRITER.

rough draft of your resume. If you answer N(o) to this prompt, indicating that you do not have a rough draft prepared, the system will ask you to make sure the printer is ready and will then go ahead and print out for you a resume outline (Fig. 6-2). You should use this outline to sketch a rough draft of the details which you want to incorporate into your resume.

Work from your rough draft and check everything, from beginning to end. Scrutinize your writing style for clarity and consistency. Refer to the list of action verbs in Chapter Three, or call them up on the computer screen by pressing **F2** whenever you are filling out a freeform section. Add, delete, or change those entries that are not powerful descriptors of your knowledge, skills, or talents. Review all dates, names, and telephone numbers for accuracy and be certain all information is positive, and relevant, to your candidacy for employment. If in doubt, cut it out!

Use your support system (family, friends, co-workers, professors, and others) as well as someone who has experience in reviewing resumes (a personnel director or human resources manager, a company recruiter, or your college placement director) to critique and assist you. Be sure to ask for feedback, not only approval. Ask your readers for specific input on how you can improve your resume, and not simply "Do you like it?" It is much better to have someone critically review your resume *before* you send it out than it is to have the employer do it when it's too late.

6.1.2   PROOFREADING

"Enjoy golf, tennis, and *bride*." "Attended University from *1890* until 1985." "Particular interest in cost and *tux* accounting." "*Coarse* in public speaking."

Resume mistakes such as these are sometimes funny—and always fatal. No matter how good you are at proofreading other people's material, you cannot do

```
                        RESUME WRITER
This is a list of items you should have before using
this program. Use this listing as a guideline to
prepare a rough draft resume.

1. PERSONAL INFORMATION
   a. Your Name
   b. Your Home/Present Address
   c. Your Telephone Number
2. EMPLOYMENT GOALS (Optional)
   A brief description (10 - 30 words) of the type
   of work you desire. This statement should reflect
   your short range plans.
3. EDUCATION
   a. Name of College(s)
   b. College City and State
   c. Degree(s) Awarded
   d. Major and Minor Concentration
   e. Overall and Major Q.P.A.
   f. Graduation Dates
   g. Depending on your Major:

       1) Courses of special value (All Majors)
       2) Honors received
       3) Certifications (Education Major)
       4) Computer Languages
       5) Computer Hardware
       6) Senior Project
       7) Directed/Independent Studies

4. WORK EXPERIENCE
   Includes: part-time employment, summer employment,
   applicable college projects, internships, and
   volunteer work. For each you should have the
   following:
   a. Company Name
   b. Company Telephone Number
   c. Your Position with the Company
   d. Job Responsibilities
5. MILITARY SERVICE (If Applicable)
   For those who have completed military
   obligations, the dates of active duty and
   rank upon discharge should be included.
6. ACTIVITIES
   Extra-curricular college and/or community
   experiences.
7. REFERENCES (Optional)
   a. First and Last Names
   b. Title
   c. Business Address
   d. Business Telephone
```

Figure 6-2 Outline for your rough draft.

your own. Because you will have invested so much time in creating your resume, your eyes may see what *should* be there rather than what *is* there. Always have someone else proofread your resume, even if you have utilized a spellchecking feature of a word processing program.

6.1.3 CHOOSING PAPER

Using a program such as THE RESUME WRITER gives you the advantage of having your information stored on a disk. The possibilities for updates, corrections, or format changes are endless. With a letter quality or laser printer, you will be able to produce a sharp, flawless document every time.

While utilizing computers to create a resume is advocated, using "computer paper" is not. Quality paper is just as important to the image of a resume as is its content. The ideal paper should have a weight of approximately 25 lbs. Suitable textures include linen finishes, rag paper, or heavy bond—anything that conveys professionalism. Stick with the standard 8½ by 11 inch page size. Legal size paper is awkward to handle and is considered inappropriate for resumes.

The preference for paper color remains white or off-white. The off-white color range includes ivory, buff, cream and a host of many other hues. Darker tans, as well as blue, gray, and other non-traditional colors, are not generally preferred by employers. White is easiest on the eye.

6.1.4 ADDITIONAL TIPS AND REMINDERS

Because these items are important, you are advised to use this section as a checklist for producing the final product.

_____ My resume is no longer than one and a half pages.

_____ My occupational objective is focused, but not too broad or too specific.

_____ I have excluded all extraneous and negative information.

_____ I have had some other competent person read over my resume to check it for errors.

_____ My resume is polished in appearance, easy to read, and error-free.

_____ I have used underlining, upper case, enlarged, or bolded words for added emphasis.

_____ I have chosen good quality white, or off-white, paper with a professional finish.

_____ My resume is the best personal commercial I can create. When it speaks for me, it says: "Here is someone who can do the job, will do the job well, and will fit in your organization."

When you have checked "yes" to all these items, turn on that printer! You have written it right, and it is time to generate your finished resume.

chapter 7

Cover Letters

LEARNING OBJECTIVES:

After reading Chapter Seven, you will have learned the mechanics of constructing effective cover letters:

- ☐ Guidelines for preparing cover letters
- ☐ Three messages for your reader
    - ☐ getting attention
    - ☐ generating interest
    - ☐ suggesting contact
- ☐ Business basics

7.1 GUIDELINES FOR PREPARING COVER LETTERS

A cover letter, also known as a letter of application, broadcast letter, or introduction letter, is an individually prepared communication mailed along with every resume you send. Cover letters are intended to relate information about your background to the needs of a specific organization, without repeating verbatim what appears on the resume.

Well done, customized cover letters will make a difference in the number of positive responses you receive as a result of your resume mail campaign. Cover letters are not necessary in situations where you will meet personally with employers. In those cases you have the advantage of verbally presenting yourself and your written document.

The cover letter is personalized, individually prepared (no Xerox or offset here), and should be addressed to a specific person by name. Anything less looks like, and is handled as, junk mail.

Covers are brief. A letter of more than a page is an automatic turn off. Follow accepted business letter guidelines when writing a cover letter. Keep words, sentences, and paragraphs short and simple, but concise. The same kind of action verbs and phrases which called attention to your merits in the resume (see listing Fig. 3-7, page 20) should be used in the cover letters.

7.2 THREE MESSAGES FOR YOUR READER

Although there may be variations, a basic cover letter has three paragraphs and three messages to convey to readers. The first paragraph indicates why the reader is receiving this information (getting attention). Paragraph two states why the candidate is appropriate or special for a position (generating interest). The final paragraph closes with what action is being requested (suggesting contact).

The following three sections elaborate on these messages and will assist you in creating the body of your cover letters.

7.2.1 GETTING ATTENTION

For starters, do your homework and find out who in the organization should receive your letter and resume. Most likely it will be someone with direct hiring power, or someone who can forward your material to an appropriate person. If you know the company, but not the exact person, telephone the organization and mention you are sending something to the personnel (or other) department. Simply ask, "To whom should I address this material?"

Using an individual's name on this correspondence personalizes your communication in a way that the printed resume could never do on its own. When you answer classified ads with only a box number and no mention of the company, you will be unable to find an exact receiver. In those instances, use a very broad salutation with no gender either stated or implied, such as "Dear Personnel Director," or "Dear Employer."

In the opening paragraph, state the source of referral, if applicable, and for what position you are applying. Mention a publication's name and date or quote a person's name if your letter is a result of such referral. Something in one of the first few sentences should indicate that you know what the company does and that you are aware of what it needs or wants to accomplish. A little research on the employer can go a long way here.

Public libraries, college career centers, bureaus of employment security, and local chambers of commerce are good sources of company information. People who work for a particular company can also serve as resources for employer research.

Targeting your letter to a specific person and indicating, or at least implying, that you know something about the organization establishes that this letter is not a form letter. You have the employer's attention!

7.2.2 GENERATING INTEREST

The next task is to communicate to the reader how your background could be valuable to the organization. Your second paragraph creates a bridge between you and the work category or specific position. State your abilities, accomplishments, or areas of expertise, with a reference to appropriate sections of your resume. Do not repeat word for word what appears on the resume. If an advertisement or other source reveals requirements or preferences which are not addressed in your resume, cover it here.

Highlight your professional qualifications to demonstrate what makes you appropriate for the job and shows what talent you have to offer. You have 'em thinking!

7.2.3 SUGGESTING CONTACT

The final step in your cover letter is to plan for follow-up. Avoid a passive close such as: "I look forward to hearing from you concerning this employment opportunity." Such a close suggests an interview at the employer's convenience. A more pro-active approach puts action in your court: "I will contact your office within the next two weeks to schedule an interview." Your final paragraph leaves a final impression with the reader. Make it strong and make it clear that you are serious about meeting to further market your candidacy for employment.

Explain when, where, and how you may be contacted or better yet, indicate that you intend to follow-up to establish personal contact. You've turned that desire into action!

7.3 BUSINESS BASICS

To make for an even more effective cover letter, follow accepted standards in preparing basic business letters. Heading, inside address, salutation, body, complimentary close, and signature appear in that order. Be sure that each cover letter is hand-signed. The address on the envelope should coincide in all particulars with the inside address.

Quality stationery is a must. Using some of the sheets you bought for printing your resume is a good idea.

When you are ready to mail your material, clip your cover letter on top of your resume. Using large manilla envelopes is prefered over business envelopes because you can send your resume and letter without folding it. If you must fold it, however, remember that a business letter is folded in thirds (Fig. 7-1). No other method is acceptable.

To help you combine these tips, refer to the following examples of well-done, customized cover letters (Figs. 7-2 and 7-3) and then proceed to Chapter Eight to find out what else you should do with your resume and letters to enhance your job search.

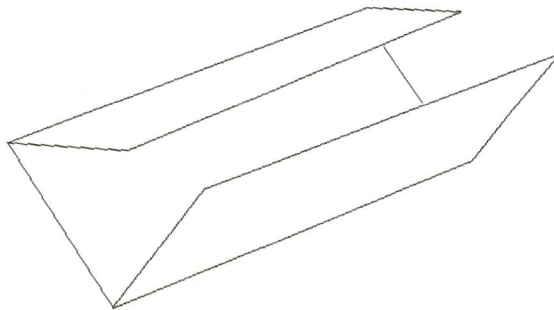

Figure 7-1   "A business letter is folded in thirds."

```
2020 Prospect Lane
Bradenville, PA 15620

October 29, 1990

Mr. Richard Tudy
Director, Human Services
TMB Corporation
358 Waterford Drive
Indianapolis, IN 46202

Dear Mr. Tudy:

I am applying for the position of program director
which you advertised in the Sunday, October 29
edition of the Indianapolis Star.

My Baccalaureate degree is in Gerontology from
California University of Pennsylvania, where I
graduated with high honors. Professionally, I have
worked as a case worker with the Washington County
Area Agency on Aging. At the Agency I planned,
directed, and evaluated comprehensive programming
for the area's senior citizen population. Enclosed
is a copy of my current résumé which expands upon my
qualifications.

I would welcome an opportunity to discuss how my
background and skills can benefit the TMB Corporation.
Early next week I will contact your office to arrange
for an interview. I look forward to meeting with you.

Sincerely,


Penny Ann Johns

enc.
```

Figure 7-2 Sample cover letter.

```
146 Ginger Avenue
Johnstown, PA 15904

May 15, 1991

Dr. Marilyn Friend
Vice President for Human Resources
Signal Communications, Inc.
P.O. Box 1227
Pittsburgh, PA 15222

Dear Dr. Friend:

Recently I picked up an issue of the Pittsburgh
Business-Times Journal and read about the work your
organization is doing in software design for the
electronics communications industry. I am very
interested in software design and, in fact, worked
a year-long internship to develop a "C" language
program to collect and process information from
highway distance measuring equipment.

A copy of my résumé is enclosed which highlights my
background in electronics and software development.
I am sure of my ability to contribute to Signal
Communications, and would welcome the opportunity
to demonstrate this ability to you.

Should my credentials and background meet your needs, I
hope you will contact me. I will make myself available
for an interview at a time convenient to you.

Sincerely,


Calvin N. Pittman

enc.
```

Figure 7-3 Sample cover letter.

chapter 8

Getting Your Message Out

LEARNING OBJECTIVES:

This chapter generates ideas for you on what you should do with your resume now that you have completed the preparation of a polished version:

- ▫ Getting your message out
  - ▫ Mail campaigns
  - ▫ Agencies and offices
  - ▫ Pounding the pavement
  - ▫ Networks and contacts
- ▫ Where do you go from here?

8.1 GETTING YOUR MESSAGE OUT

Your resume and letters will only be as effective as the quality of your marketing and distribution plan. You work too long and too diligently on creating your resume to take chances with its effectiveness. Career development specialists often speak of a "hidden job market" and it is important to learn how to tap into this market to uncover employment possibilities.

Resume and letter writing are part of a communication process. If you understand the details and nuances of how people communicate, you will have a clearer idea of how to plan your job search strategy.

Let's look first at some of the traditional job search methods.

8.1.1   MAIL CAMPAIGNS

The shotgun approach, or mass mail approach, is the least effective method of submitting your resume for consideration. With shotgunning, you target a large number of employers to receive your resume. The target group may come from a resource directory, an association list, or even a telephone directory.

Shotgunning is good for the economy (it produces paper, postage, jobs for mail sorters and carriers, more paper, more postage, and so on), but it is not good for your job search, or trees for that matter!

The numbers game is definitely against you. While there are all kinds of statistics on how many resumes you must shotgun to get one interview, in terms of time and expense, "It ain't worth it!"

If you decide to use a shotgun approach, one way to improve your chances is to follow-up your mailings with telephone calls and thank you letters. One week after sending your resumes and cover letters, contact the recipients by telephone to reaffirm interest, highlight qualifications, request interviews, and stress gratitude. Regardless of the phone conversation outcome, immediately send a written thank you as well. To some extent this telemarketing strategy will enhance your chances of being considered for interviews.

A second mail approach is that of answering announcements or advertisements of job vacancies. In some cases job hunters will be successful in securing employment by using classified advertisements as a source for submitting resumes for consideration.

You should be aware, however, that some vacancies which appear in print do not represent actual openings. Some vacancies are already scheduled to be filled and employers simply list positions to fulfill affirmative action or equal employment opportunity requirements. Other employers decide to test the market for available labor when they post non-existent jobs, hoping to collect a reference pool of resumes. And some jobs which end up in print are simply hard to fill, either because they are low-paying or highly-skilled, have undesirable hours or conditions, or have some combination of these characteristics.

Again, including telephone follow-up after answering vacancy announcements will improve your odds.

8.1.2   AGENCIES AND OFFICES

State employment services, private employment agencies, and college placement offices are available as resources to job hunters.

A state's bureau of employment services will attempt to line you up with prospective employers who have listed openings with them. This service is provided at no cost to you, or to the employer. If you decide to take advantage of a local employment office, you (and your resume) must clearly identify the type of positions you are seeking. Unless you do so, you may end up being processed as a "miscellaneous" applicant. There are no employers who contact agencies and ask for assistance in filling a miscellaneous position—employers have specific needs and want specific applicants for their openings.

Private employment agencies, on the other hand, are in business to make a profit. Either the company, or you, will pay fees for private agency services. It may not be obvious, but even a company-paid fee may end up costing *you*. An employer is likely to take the "fee" off the top of the salary range for the position. Stories abound about applicants having negative and costly experiences with private agencies. You are best advised to only use private agencies as a last resort, after you have exhausted all other methods of job hunting.

Universities, colleges, and schools provide job search assistance to their graduates through placement or career centers. If you are still in school, be sure to avail yourself of this resource. Career Services personnel at most schools express concern that all too few students take advantage of the job search services they are entitled to. Most offices also provide help for alumni.

Other traditional strategies that involve using your resume are:

- computerized resume services,
- federal listings,
- management consultants,
- and the yellow pages of phone books.

Don't fall into the trap of thinking that these mass-mail strategies constitute an effective job search campaign. Jobs in print represent a small percentage of work that is actually available. Also, employers receive quantities of unsolicited resumes and letters weekly and may not even read your material when it arrives. Intelligently mail out your resume, but look to other non-traditional methods of seeking employment to facilitate your hire.

Non-traditional job-search methods are direct, specific, and require persistence. The following are examples of non-traditional methods that really work.

8.1.3 POUNDING THE PAVEMENT

The job seeker who sits back and waits for the mail to arrive or the phone to ring is conducting a passive job search. An active search requires personal contact. Nothing will increase the effectiveness of your resume like a personal delivery. Because your resume is a written communication, it is limited in its ability to convey messages about your appearance, enthusiasm, confidence, business etiquette and so on.

Delivering your resume in person gives you a chance to make a first impression *and* affords an opportunity for you to verbally sell your abilities and talents. In such a cold-calling approach, your resume serves as your calling card.

Will employers take the time to talk to you? If surveyed, they would probably say they do not have the time to see walk-ins. In practice, however, employers (like the rest of us) usually enjoy talking about their jobs and their organizations with others who show such an interest.

What if you can't get beyond receptionists? Ask to speak to the appropriate person (related to your career interest) in the company. If that person is not available, request an appointment at another time. Seek additional information if you are unable to get what you initially requested. Ask for advice. Ask if you may leave your resume, even if they do not have current openings. Ask for other names or resources. Thank them for helping you.

Most employers value the impressions and opinions of their clerical staff when it comes to judging people, including prospective job applicants.

8.1.4 NETWORKS AND CONTACTS

The most effective job search method continues to be developing a network of people who know what kind of job you want and that you are available. Your contacts, or network system, should include everyone you can think of and everyone they can think of. Initially, you should try for 60–75 leads. If not fruitful after a period of time (whatever you have established as a realistic time limit), you should revise and expand your network system. Every member of your network should have a copy (or copies) of your resume.

Suggested contacts could include: family members, friends, neighbors, former co-workers, former employers, parents' friends, college professors or advisors, clergy, folks who sell you insurance, cut your hair, deliver your mail, serve you lunch, provide medical or dental services, and so on. As you can see, this means almost everyone who is in a position to see and talk to other people.

The majority of your most productive job search leads will come out of your communications with other people. Don't keep your job hunt a secret!

There are additional non-traditional strategies for job seekers to consider including job clubs, volunteering to create your own position, telemarketing, and others. The list is only limited by your creativity and imagination. Remember that your resume won't do you any good if it sits on your desk. You have to do something with it. Be motivated, look for new ideas, be persistent, and get your message out!

Don't keep your job hunt a secret!

8.2   WHERE DO YOU GO FROM HERE?

Congratulations! By reading Chapters One through Eight you have established a solid foundational understanding of writing a resume. You have, in essence, a "map" of THE RESUME WRITER software. Having a map makes a journey easier and you can see where you are going. Although THE RESUME WRITER will not take you through the final steps of interviewing and negotiating job offers, you will be well on your way to finding a job that is right for you. Your skills, competencies, and objectives will be clear. Writing your resume *right* is the first part of your job search process. Good luck!

part II

USING THE
RESUME WRITER

chapter 9

Creating Your Resume

LEARNING OBJECTIVES:

In this chapter you will step through the process of using the computer to put together your resume. This includes from preparing your rough draft through to collecting all the data for the various entries and storing them on the computer system:

- Tips for the first time user of THE RESUME WRITER
- The importance of the rough draft
- Using the menus
- What to do if you make a mistake or change your mind
- Deciding what resume format to use
- THE RESUME WRITER speaks for itself—just follow the directions
- How to handle the Job Objective and other Freeform sections
- Don't expect to get it right first time—you can always change things later

9.1 TIPS FOR THE FIRST TIME USER OF THE RESUME WRITER

Starting Out with THE RESUME WRITER.

To begin working with THE RESUME WRITER, turn on your PC. After a while, a prompt will appear on the screen, either **A:\>** or **C:\>**, which waits for some response from you. If the prompt is **A:\>**, make sure THE RESUME WRITER disk is in drive A. If the prompt is **C:\>**, and you have THE RESUME WRITER installed on your hard drive in the root directory, you are ready to boot (call up) THE RESUME WRITER.[1] If neither of these situations is the case on your PC, you either know what you are doing, so there is no problem, **OR** you're not sure what to do next, in which case you should read Appendix A or ask for advice from someone who knows their way around the IBM PC.

Let us assume you are ready to go. All you do is type the two letters **RW** and press the **Enter** (or **Return**) key. Uppercase or lowercase letters don't make any difference. After a few seconds the introductory screen for THE RESUME WRITER will appear.

Read PART I of This Book Carefully.

Writing a good resume is a crucial first step in your job search. It is not something you can toss off without preparation and careful planning. PART I of this book is full of wisdom about the process of writing a good resume. Take time to read it first.

Read Appendix A If You Are a First Time Computer User.

Appendix A is for the first time computer user. If you fit into this category, Appendix A will explain everything you need to know about using the various parts of the computer hardware, as well as how to get started in THE RESUME WRITER.

Take Your Time.

Writing a resume is a painstaking task. It isn't easy to put together a good one. Take whatever time is necessary to **Write It Right**. The investment in time now will pay off in the long run.

Be Patient.

Especially if you are a first time user of the IBM PC computer system. It can be frustrating familiarizing yourself with a new piece of software such as THE RESUME WRITER, let alone adjusting to a new hardware environment. Although the software has been carefully crafted to simplify the whole process of capturing the data for your resume, and although it has been already well received by many users, you should nonetheless expect a certain amount of "strangeness," in just the same way as you would expect a new off-the-rack suit to be just a tad uncomfortable at first. After all, THE RESUME WRITER was not tailor-made to suit your *unique* individual needs.

Quality Is in the Details.

If you want to produce the best resume, you should attend to the details. Spelling, punctuation, grammar, choice of words, and selection of page layout, are all very important. They are also your responsibility. THE RESUME WRITER will help

---

[1] Should this last sentence be incomprehensible to you, and the prompt on the screen is indeed C:\>, all is not lost. But you will need to seek help from someone who is familiar with the IBM PC and PC/MS-DOS. There are plenty of such wonderful people around.

you a great deal, but it cannot do everything for you. If you feel unsure about your abilities in these areas of the art of writing you should not hesitate to seek help from those you know, such as a teacher, who have the expertise.

9.2 THE IMPORTANCE OF THE ROUGH DRAFT

When you first boot THE RESUME WRITER you will be presented with a screen (see Fig. 9-1a) which will ask you if you have prepared a rough draft of your resume before you begin.

If you have not, you should answer **N** (No) to this question. The system will then go ahead and print out for you an outline which will itemize the kind of data that you will be required to supply for your resume (Fig. 9-1b). You should, of course, make sure the printer is turned on. But just in case you forget, THE RESUME WRITER always checks such things for you and will warn you about anything that may need your attention.

When you are preparing your rough draft, questions will undoubtedly arise that will cause you to want to think more carefully about your resume than you perhaps expected. You might even feel that you should seek help from a career counsellor. If you are a student at a college, this is a very wise thing to do. What is more, your school's career counsellors will be delighted to see you. Nine out of ten college counsellors are mystified that more students don't avail themselves of the services available in the Career Services Office.

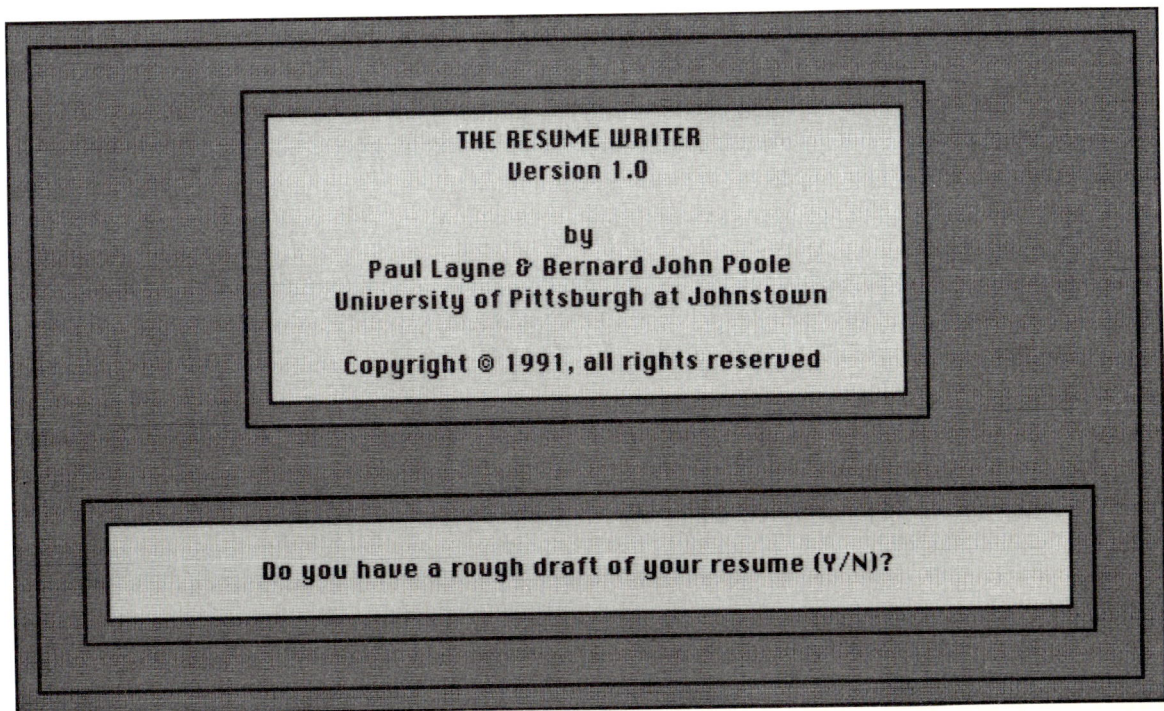

```
              THE RESUME WRITER
                 Version 1.0


                      by
         Paul Layne & Bernard John Poole
       University of Pittsburgh at Johnstown

         Copyright © 1991, all rights reserved




        Do you have a rough draft of your resume (Y/N)?
```

Figure 9-1a   Introductory screen for THE RESUME WRITER.

```
                        RESUME WRITER

This is a list of items you should have before using
this program. Use this listing as a guideline to
prepare a rough draft resume.

  1.  PERSONAL INFORMATION
      a.  Your Name
      b.  Your Home/Present Address
      c.  Your Telephone Number
  2.  EMPLOYMENT GOALS (Optional)
      A brief description (10 - 30 words) of the type
      of work you desire. This statement should reflect
      your short range plans.
  3.  EDUCATION
      a.  Name of College(s)
      b.  College City and State
      c.  Degree(s) Awarded
      d.  Major and Minor Concentration
      e.  Overall and Major Q.P.A.
      f.  Graduation Dates
      g.  Depending on your Major:

          1)  Courses of special value (All Majors)
          2)  Honors received
          3)  Certifications (Education Major)
          4)  Computer Languages
          5)  Computer Hardware
          6)  Senior Project
          7)  Directed/Independent Studies

  4.  WORK EXPERIENCE
      Includes: part-time employment, summer employment,
      applicable college projects, internships, and
      volunteer work. For each you should have the
      following:
      a.  Company Name
      b.  Company Telephone Number
      c.  Your Position with the Company
      d.  Job Responsibilities
  5.  MILITARY SERVICE (If Applicable)
      For those who have completed military
      obligations, the dates of active duty and
      rank upon discharge should be included.
  6.  ACTIVITIES
      Extra-curricular college and/or community
      experiences.
  7.  REFERENCES (Optional)
      a.  First and Last Names
      b.  Title
      c.  Business Address
      d.  Business Telephone
```

Figure 9-1b Outline for your rough draft.

9.3   USING THE MENUS

Once you have prepared your rough draft you are ready to enter the data for your resume into the computer. Assuming that you have gone ahead and booted the software, and told the system that you have indeed prepared your rough draft, you will be presented with the Main Menu screen (Fig. 9-2a).

THE RESUME WRITER is menu-driven. So you will select what you want to do at any point in time from a menu of options available to you on the screen. You have two alternative ways of choosing an option on a menu:

1. you can **EITHER** use the arrow keys on the numeric keypad on the right hand side of the keyboard to move up and down the menus; this has the advantage, as you can see (Fig. 9-2a), of causing an explanation for each menu item you select to pop up on the screen so you know in advance what the outcome of each selection will be; once you have thus **Chosen** a menu item, you **Select** the item by pressing the **Return** key;

2. **OR** you can simply press the first letter of the menu item you want, and the system will immediately go to that section of THE RESUME WRITER.

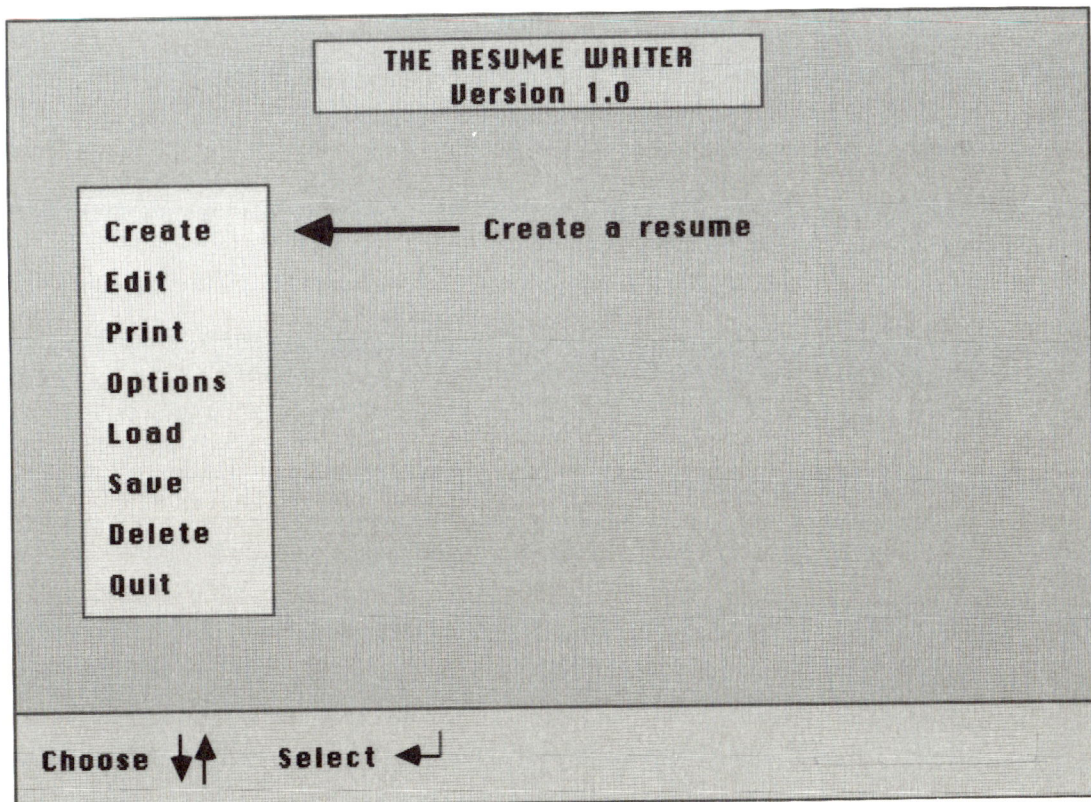

```
        ┌─────────────────────────────┐
        │     THE RESUME WRITER       │
        │       Version 1.0           │
        └─────────────────────────────┘


   ┌──────────────┐
   │ Create       │ ◄────── Create a resume
   │ Edit         │
   │ Print        │
   │ Options      │
   │ Load         │
   │ Save         │
   │ Delete       │
   │ Quit         │
   └──────────────┘


   Choose ↓↑    Select ↵
```

Figure 9-2a   The main menu.

9.4   WHAT TO DO IF YOU MAKE A MISTAKE OR
CHANGE YOUR MIND

If ever you make the wrong selection from a menu, or if you enter some data that you're not happy with, you can change your mind by pressing the **ESC** key. Pressing the **ESC** key will always take you back to the previous task that you did. In fact, the **ESC** key will allow you to go all the way back to the beginning of THE RESUME WRITER just by repeatedly pressing it.

Bear in mind that if you ESC all the way out of the Create option and back to the Main Menu you will lose all the data you may have so far entered. THE RESUME WRITER will, however, warn you about this before you elect to ESC to the Main Menu.

You should also know that THE RESUME WRITER will allow you many opportunities to edit your work. Methods for doing this will be explained later in Chapter Eleven.

In order to create a resume from scratch, you will select **Create** from the **Main Menu**. Either use the arrow keys to highlight the word **Create**, and then press the **Return** key, or just press C.

9.5   DECIDING WHAT RESUME FORMAT TO USE

When you select **Create** from the **Main Menu**, you notice that another menu pops up on the screen (Fig. 9-2b). This is the **Resume Format** menu, and it allows you to choose from three different resume formats, all of which are

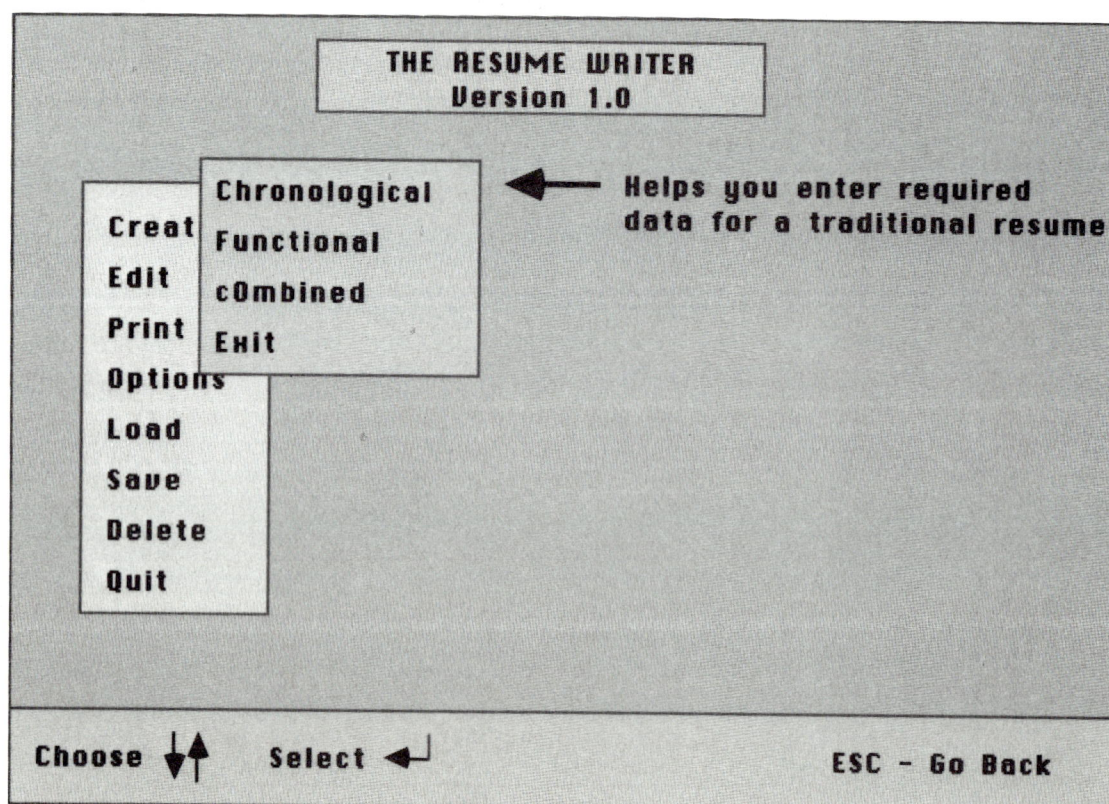

THE RESUME WRITER
Version 1.0

Creat | **Chronological**
Edit | **Functional**
Print | **cOmbined**
Options | **Exit**
Load
Save
Delete
Quit

◄— Helps you enter required data for a traditional resume

Choose ↓↑   Select ◄┘   ESC - Go Back

Figure 9-2b   Resume format menu.

extensively discussed in PART I of this book. So you have probably decided by now which format you plan to use.

Of course, you will be able to change your mind if you find that the format you choose turns out to be inappropriate. It's quite possible, also, that you will want to use one format for one job application, and another format for something else. The beauty of THE RESUME WRITER is that it makes it easy for you to customize according to your needs.

Whichever resume format you choose (by selecting it from the **Resume Format** menu), the system will then proceed to step you through the process of data acquisition item by item. This is where the time you spent up front preparing your rough draft will pay off. This is especially true of either the Functional format or the Combination format, because the data required for these two formats is not nearly as cut and dried as that required for the Chronological resume.

9.6 THE RESUME WRITER SPEAKS FOR ITSELF—JUST FOLLOW THE DIRECTIONS

Keying in all the data for your resume is quite a time consuming process. However, it is, on the whole, self-explanatory. There are help screens along the way that explain what you will need to enter next. There is also, as already mentioned, an explanation of each menu item, which pops up on the screen as you browse through a menu. Furthermore, each screen has specific prompts which leave no doubt as to what you must type in each time. Fig. 9-3, for example, is

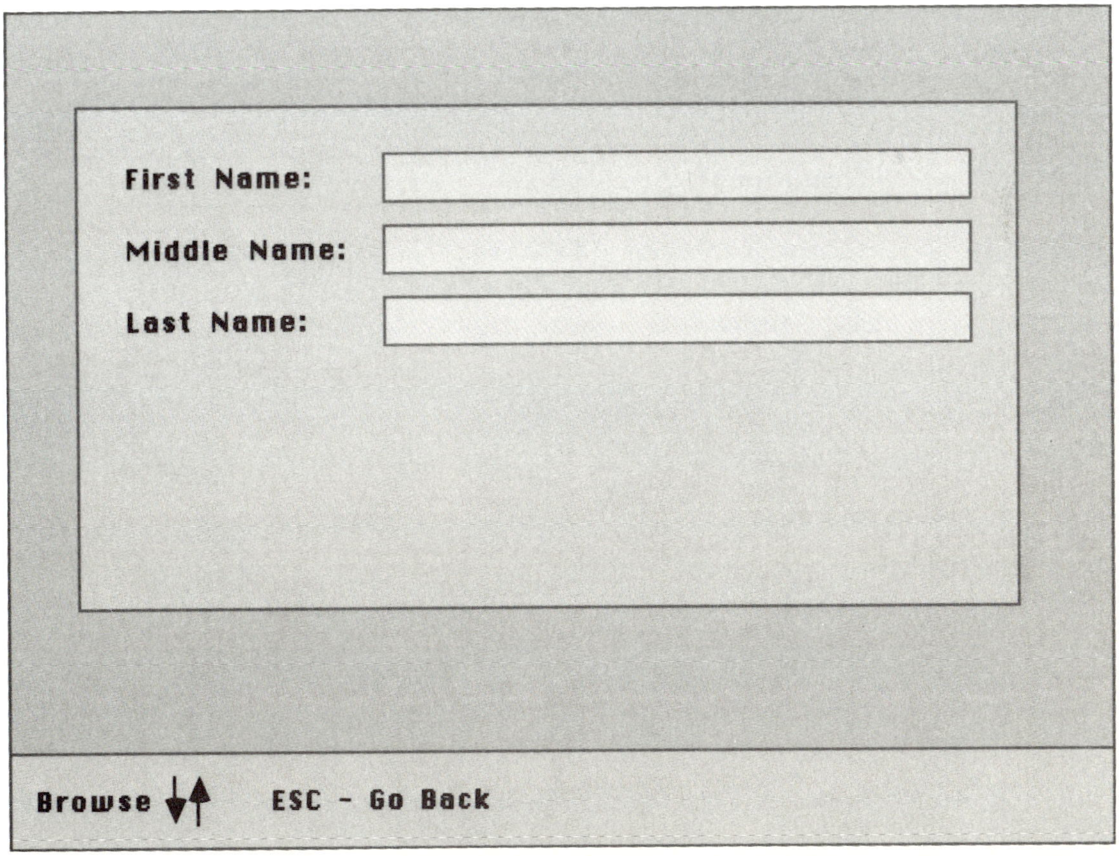

Figure 9-3 Typical data entry screen.

the data entry screen you will see first no matter what resume format you choose.

The cursor waits for you to key in your data in each data entry box. When you are done entering an item, you will press **Return**, and the cursor will move down to the next data entry box.

After entering the data for any particular screen you will be given the opportunity to make corrections before going on to the next screen (Fig. 9-4). And, of course, you will be able to **ESC** back at any time to any previous screen should you wish to check what you have done, or should you want to make any changes.

If, as you review the data that you have just entered for a particular screen, you decide that you *do* want to make a change here and there before going on to the next screen, you will respond **N** to the prompt:

Is the above information correct   Y/N   ?

and THE RESUME WRITER will present another menu (an Edit menu) at the bottom of the screen which will allow you to select which item it is you would like to correct (Fig. 9-5).

Eventually, you will move on to the next screen by responding **Y** to the prompt which asks you if all the information on the screen is correct.

Sometimes, you will be entering data into a field which has a predictable set of values. For example, a telephone Area Code always has three digits. Anything else would be incorrect. This is also true of a State abbreviation where

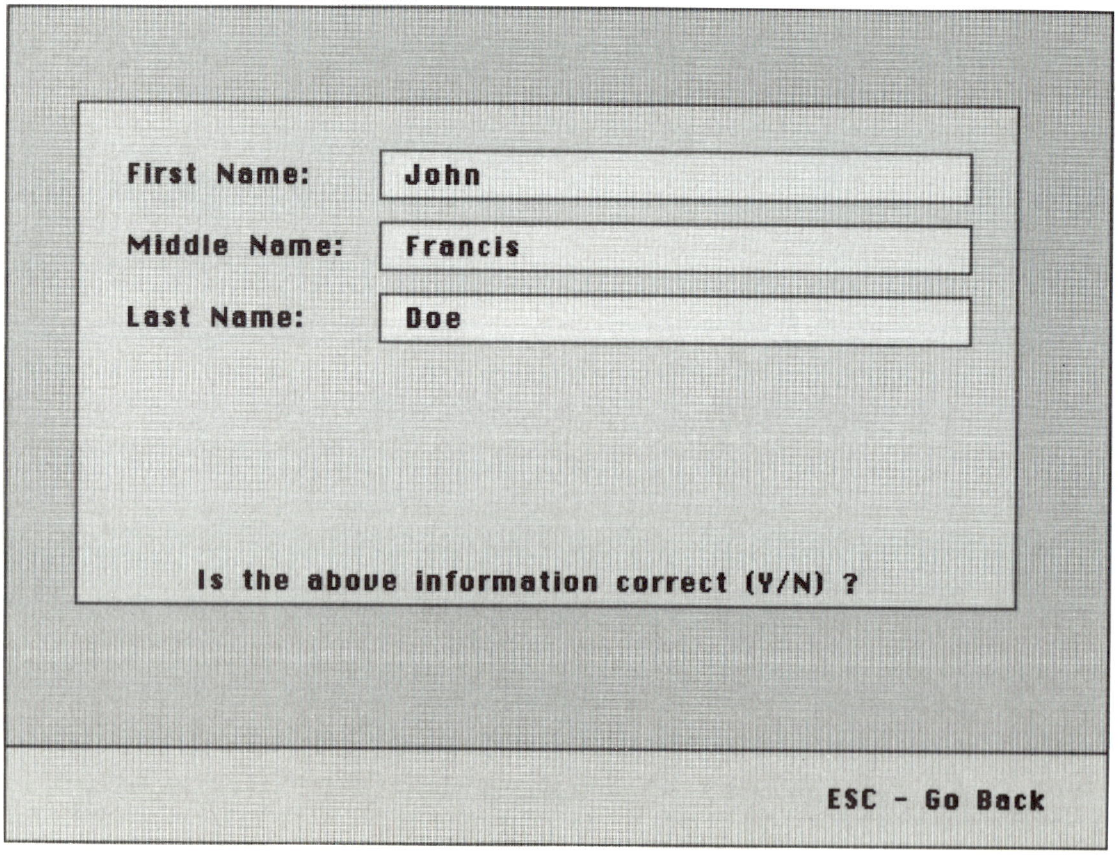

Figure 9-4 Data validation prompt.

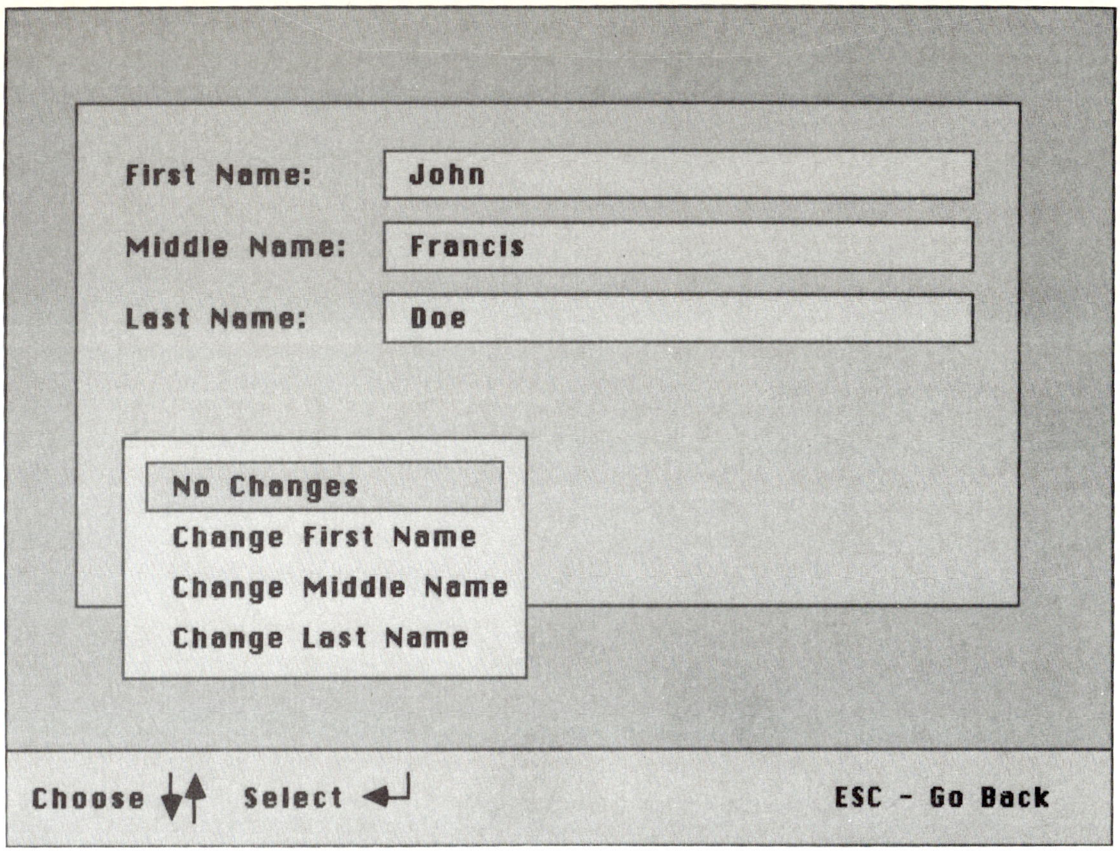

Figure 9-5   Typical edit menu.

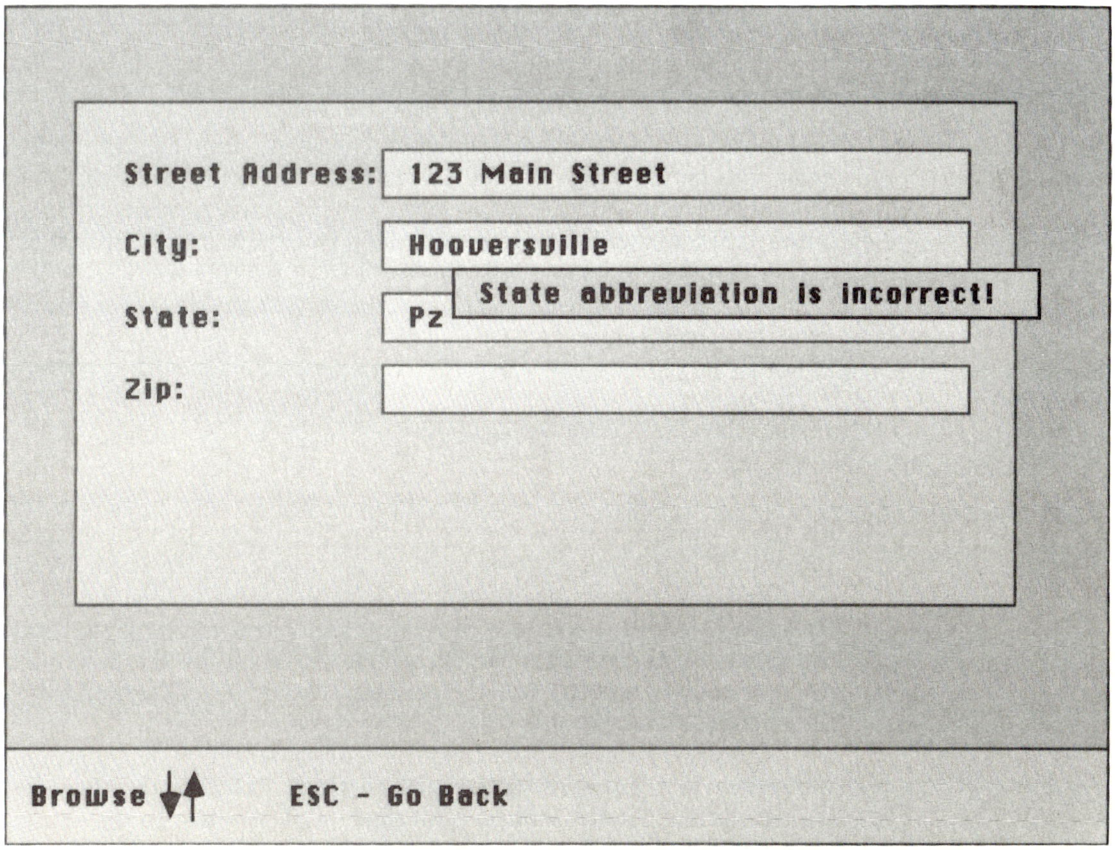

Figure 9-6   Warning of incorrect state abbreviation.

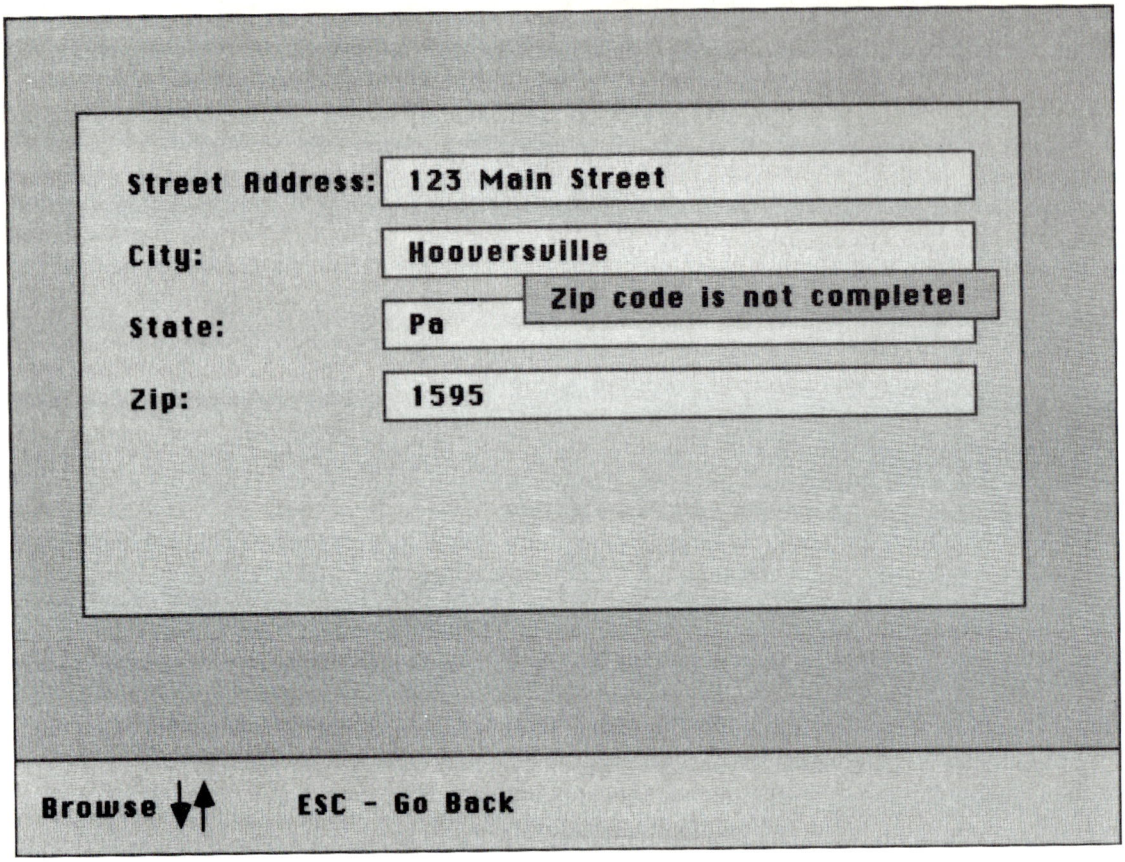

Figure 9-7 Warning of incorrect zip code.

there are just fifty correct entries. Likewise, for the Zip Code a correct entry will be made up of either five digits or nine digits. Nothing else will do. THE RESUME WRITER has been programmed to watch over you as you enter data for such fields in order to help you avoid making mistakes (Figs. 9-6 and 9-7).

This pattern of processing will repeat itself until you have entered all the data for your resume.

9.7 HOW TO HANDLE THE JOB OBJECTIVE AND OTHER FREEFORM SECTIONS

For the Functional resume, and for the Functional parts of a Combination resume, you will make extensive use of what is known in THE RESUME WRITER as a **freeform** entry area. As you can see (Fig. 9-8), this is a larger data entry box than usual. It allows you to type in six lines of text any way you want. The Job Objective is a typical freeform entry item; so would be the description of your job responsibilities in the Work Experience section. All of the data entry boxes for the Functional resume are of the freeform type.

Curiously enough, these freeform entries, which leave you at liberty to say whatever you like, are often the most difficult to complete. They are certainly the entries that require most careful thought. They are also the entries that will be most likely to show off your writing skills, and your care for correctness of

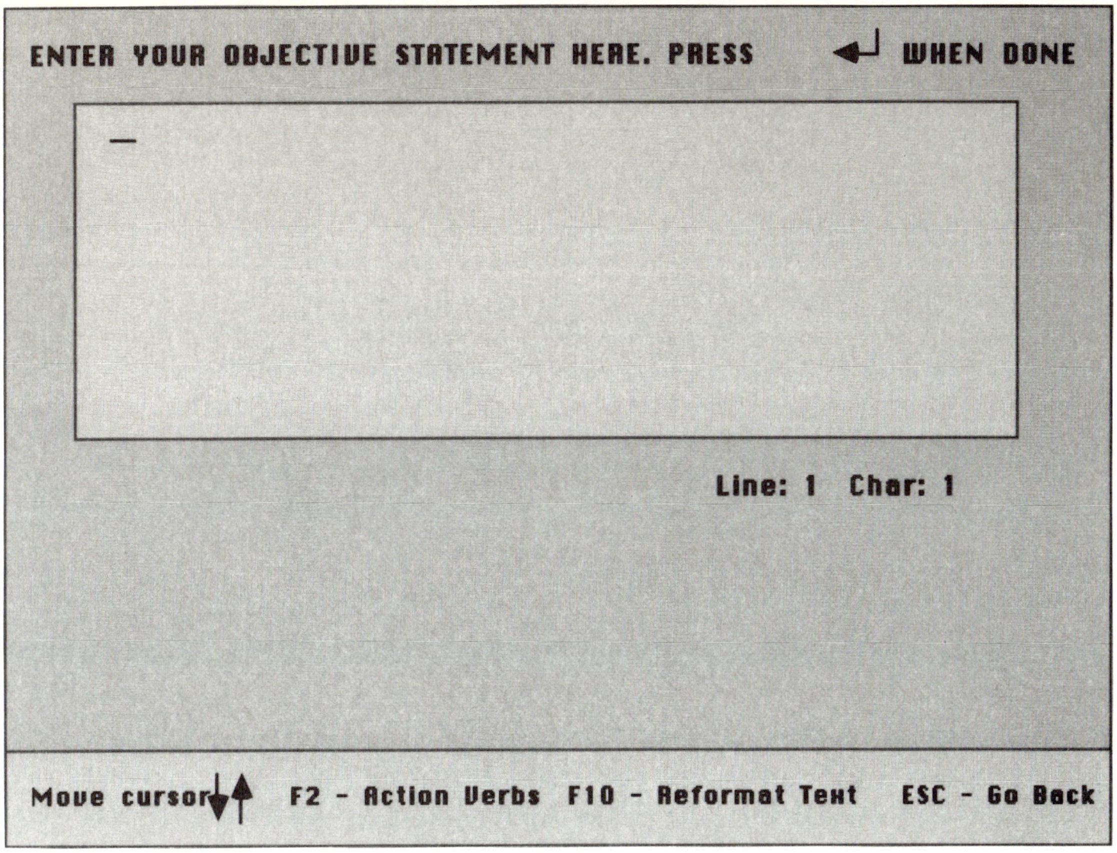

Figure 9-8 Typical freeform data entry area.

detail in written communication. You should therefore give these sections the attention they deserve. Planning, once again, is the name of the game.

As you can see from the help bar at the bottom of the screen in Fig. 9-8, you can use certain keys on the keyboard to help you complete the freeform sections. Let's take them one by one (see Figs. 9-9 and 9-10).

The Cursor Move Keys:

- The cursor move keys are located on the right hand side of the keyboard. In the freeform sections you can use these keys to go left, right, up a line, or down a line anywhere in the six line text window.
- The **Home** key will send the cursor to the beginning of the line it is currently on.
- The **End** key will send the cursor to the end of the line it is currently on.

The F2 Key:

- This function key (located on the left of the keyboard) will cause a set of **Action Verbs** to be displayed on the screen beneath the freeform data entry window. Good resume writing is clear and direct. Action verbs make a stronger statement and convey the sense that you can get the job done. You may find these action verbs useful when putting together your thoughts for any of the freeform sections, such as your Job Objective.

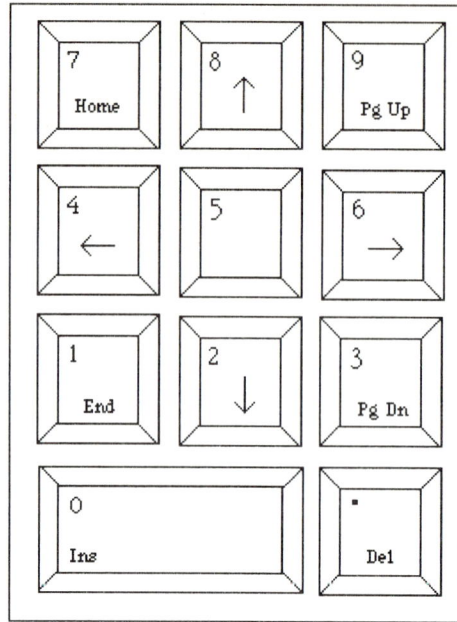

Figure 9-9   The numeric keypad.

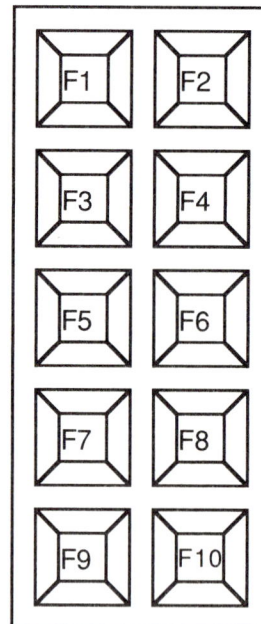

Figure 9-10   The function keypad.

The F 10 Key:

- This key should be used when you want to re-organize, or reformat, your text after you have made changes to it. For example, if you removed a word or two from a line, there will be an unnecessarily large gap at the end of the line. Because you may intend such a gap, THE RESUME WRITER does not automatically rearrange your text to fill it in. Instead you are given the tools (the F10 key) to reformat at your discretion. Pressing the F10 key will cause the text to be reformatted to take on a more normal paragraph appearance by filling in each line in the freeform window. Chapter Eleven on the subject of editing explains this function in more detail.

You may well ask why you are limited to just six lines in the freeform sections. The answer is simple: the briefer your resume the better. You get no extra points for verbosity. If the reader cannot scan the material in your resume in under 20 seconds, it will probably not get read at all.

THE RESUME WRITER has been designed to help you write an *effective* resume. You should therefore accept this six line limitation as a help rather than a hindrance, and work within its restrictions.

However, there may be special circumstances where you absolutely must use more than the allotted six lines. If this is the case, read Chapter Thirteen, The Power User. There you will learn how to use THE RESUME WRITER hand in hand with your favorite word processor. This will allow you freedom to create whatever resume you please.

But remember, freedom means responsibility. You should not take this option unless you already know what constitutes a quality resume. It will be up to you to do the necessary research, seek all necessary advice, in order to protect your own interest of effectively presenting your personal commercial to the world of work.

An excellent starting point for this research will be to read PART I of this text if you have not already done so. Then you should run through THE RESUME WRITER at least once since it will act as a tutorial in the fundamentals of good resume writing. By the time you have done this you will have a good idea of what resume writing involves, and thus will be better able to take advantage of the Power User feature of the software.

9.8 DON'T EXPECT TO GET IT RIGHT FIRST TIME—YOU CAN ALWAYS MAKE CHANGES LATER

The ease with which you can correct your work is a major asset of THE RESUME WRITER. Since it is a dedicated word processor (a word processor dedicated to the processing of a resume), it has all the advantages of a word processor, not least of which is that it significantly improves the quality of your writing by facilitating the editorial function—which is the subject of Chapter Eleven.

But before you do anything, you must save all the work you have done so far. That, and other file management functions such as loading files and deleting files, will be the subject of the next chapter.

chapter 10

Managing Your Resume Files on Disk

LEARNING OBJECTIVES:

This chapter explains how to maintain order among your resume files on disk. You will learn how to save resume versions on THE RESUME WRITER diskette itself, or on other diskettes. You will also learn how to load, or retrieve, your resume from the disk on which you saved it. You will learn how to delete unwanted resume files from your disks. Finally, you will learn how to make backup copies.

- □ Saving the first version of your resume on THE RESUME WRITER disk
- □ Choosing appropriate names for different versions of your resume
- □ Making a backup copy of your resume on another disk
- □ Loading your resume from THE RESUME WRITER diskette
- □ Viewing a list of the resume files you have on disk
- □ Deleting files from THE RESUME WRITER diskette
- □ Making a backup of the working copy of THE RESUME WRITER

10.1 SAVING THE FIRST VERSION OF YOUR RESUME ON THE RESUME WRITER DISKETTE

THE RESUME WRITER has been designed to be easy to use by people who may not have had much experience using a computer. Consequently, just in case you may not know what to do, your work will be automatically saved any time you **Exit** the **Create** (described in Chapter Nine) or **Edit** (described in

Chapter Eleven) options from the Main Menu (see Fig. 10-1). The version of your resume you have been working on will be saved on THE RESUME WRITER diskette or directory under the name **RESUME.DAT.** This file will always contain the latest version of your resume, that is to say, the version that you were last working on.

When you want to keep different versions of your resume, which is quite likely if you are customizing your resume to meet the needs of applications to different organizations, you must select the **Save** option from the **Main Menu** (see Fig. 10-2) after you are done creating or editing. The Save option will step you through the naming of the new file to which the resume is to be saved.

Whenever you create a completely new resume, or edit an existing resume, the system will leave it up to you as to whether or not you want to save the resume in its own file on disk. This is because you may not *want* to save a new version. So the decision is left up to you. However, in case you simply forget to name your new resume file, the system will warn you that you have not done so when you choose to quit THE RESUME WRITER. Thus there is less likelihood you will lose all the good work you have done!

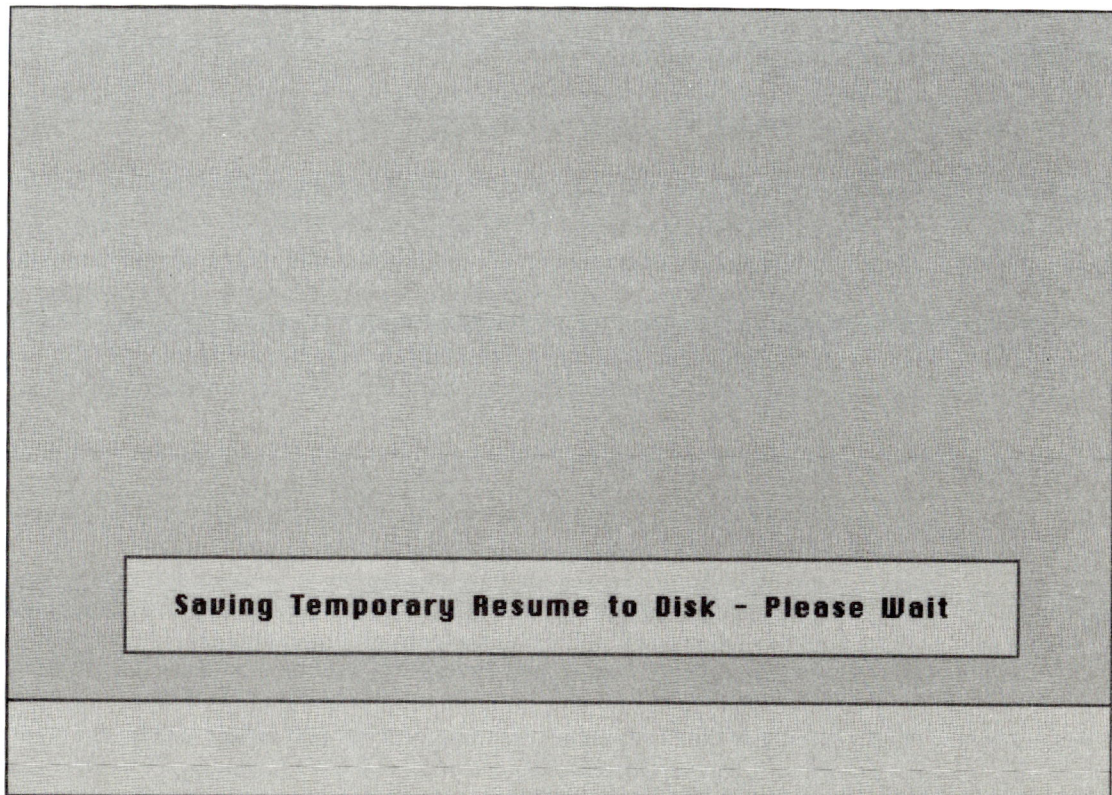

Figure 10-1 Saving your resume to the file RESUME.DAT.

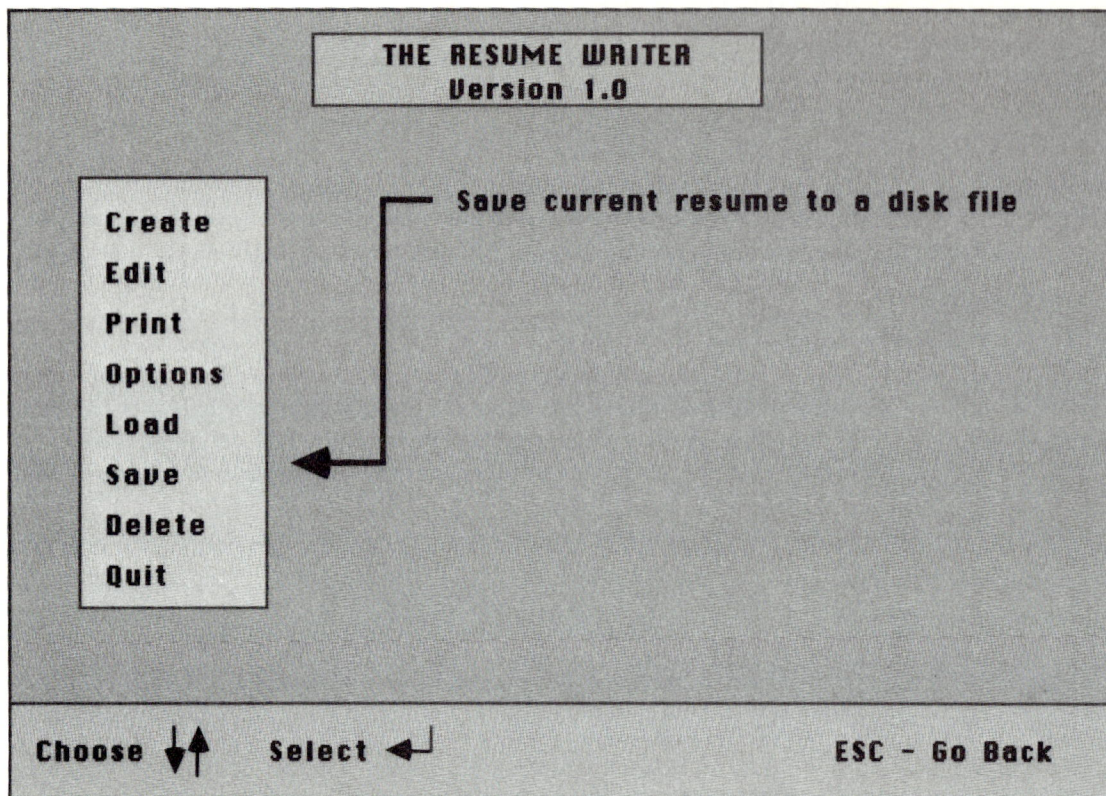

Figure 10-2   The save option from the main menu.

10.2   CHOOSING APPROPRIATE NAMES FOR DIFFERENT VERSIONS OF YOUR RESUME

As Shakespeare wrote: "What's in a name?" Well, when it comes to keeping some kind of order in your life, how you name things is very important indeed. More time than you would imagine is lost working at a computer because of the thoughtless way in which files and data are named. This section will help you make good decisions about this aspect of using a computer.

It's quite possible you may want more than one version of your resume. You may have made changes because of the requirements of one particular company to which you will be sending this new version. But the earlier version may still be relevant and you may want to keep it. So what you want to do is come up with another name for the new version of your resume so it will be saved separately from the previous one.

This is much like keeping your work in a file cabinet. In order to keep things organized you would open up a new manila folder with its own identifying tab that clearly indicates the contents of the folder.

In order to save a new version of your resume on THE RESUME WRITER diskette, you will select the **Save** option from the **Main Menu**, which is the first menu that appears on the screen when you boot the software. The system will then prompt you for the name of the new resume that you want to save (Fig. 10-3).

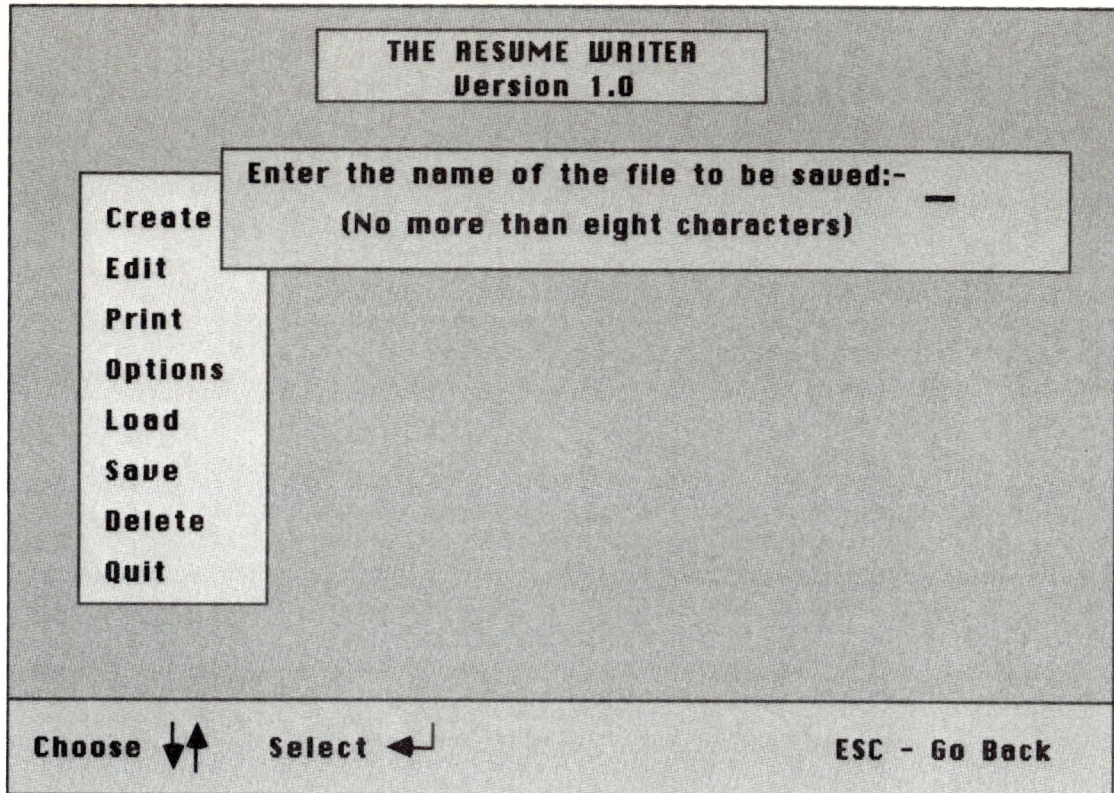

Figure 10-3 Prompt for the name of the file to be saved.

If you were to use a name which you have already used for an earlier version of your resume, you would erase the version with that name that you already have on your diskette.

As Fig. 10-4 illustrates, the **name** you give a resume file is actually the address or location on the disk where the computer system stores the file. So if you have already saved a version with the same name as the one you are about to save, the system, if you allow this to happen, will store it in the same place on the disk and erase the previous one by writing over it.

THE RESUME WRITER will, for this reason, warn you about this, and give you the option of changing your mind (Fig. 10-5). If you *do* change your mind, you will choose a name that is different from any other name you have already used for one of your resume versions. On the other hand, you may well want to replace the earlier version with an updated version that incorporates changes you have made. In that case you will tell the system to go ahead and do just that.

What *is* an appropriate name for a new version of your resume?

First of all, you *must* obey certain rules of the operating system (MS-DOS). These are easy enough to learn:

1. The name you choose for the file *must begin with a number (0–9) or a letter of the alphabet* (upper or lower case), and should be *made up of only letters of the alphabet or the digits 0 thru 9;*

2. The name must be *no more than 8 (eight) characters in length;*

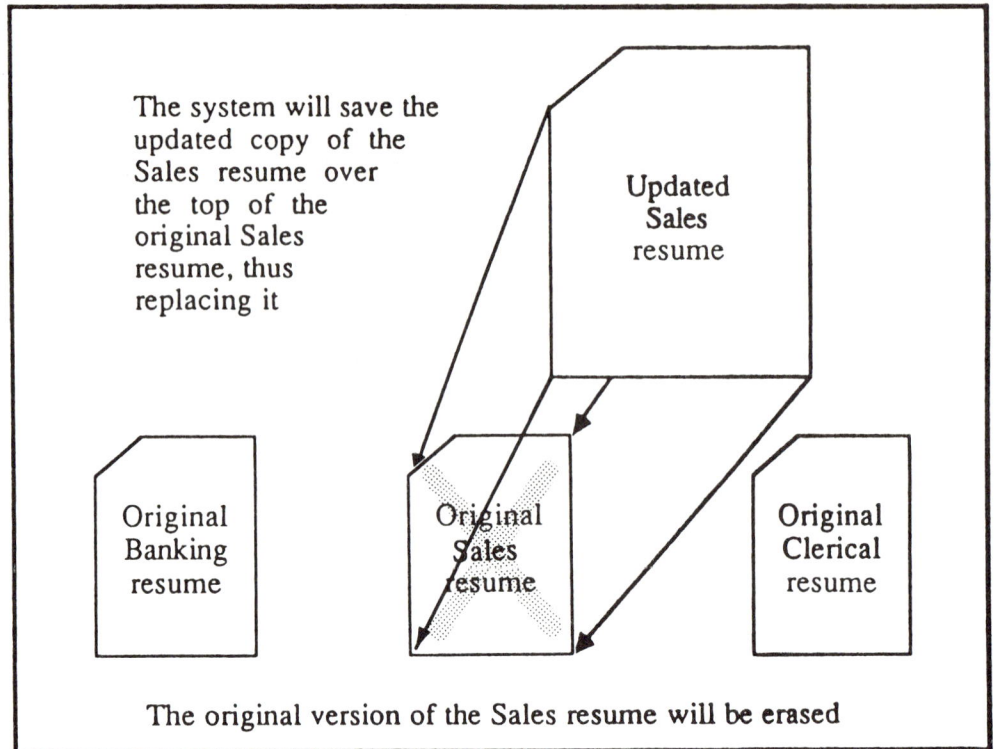

The system will save the updated copy of the Sales resume over the top of the original Sales resume, thus replacing it

Updated Sales resume

Original Banking resume

Original Sales resume

Original Clerical resume

The original version of the Sales resume will be erased

Figure 10-4 Overwriting a file with the same name.

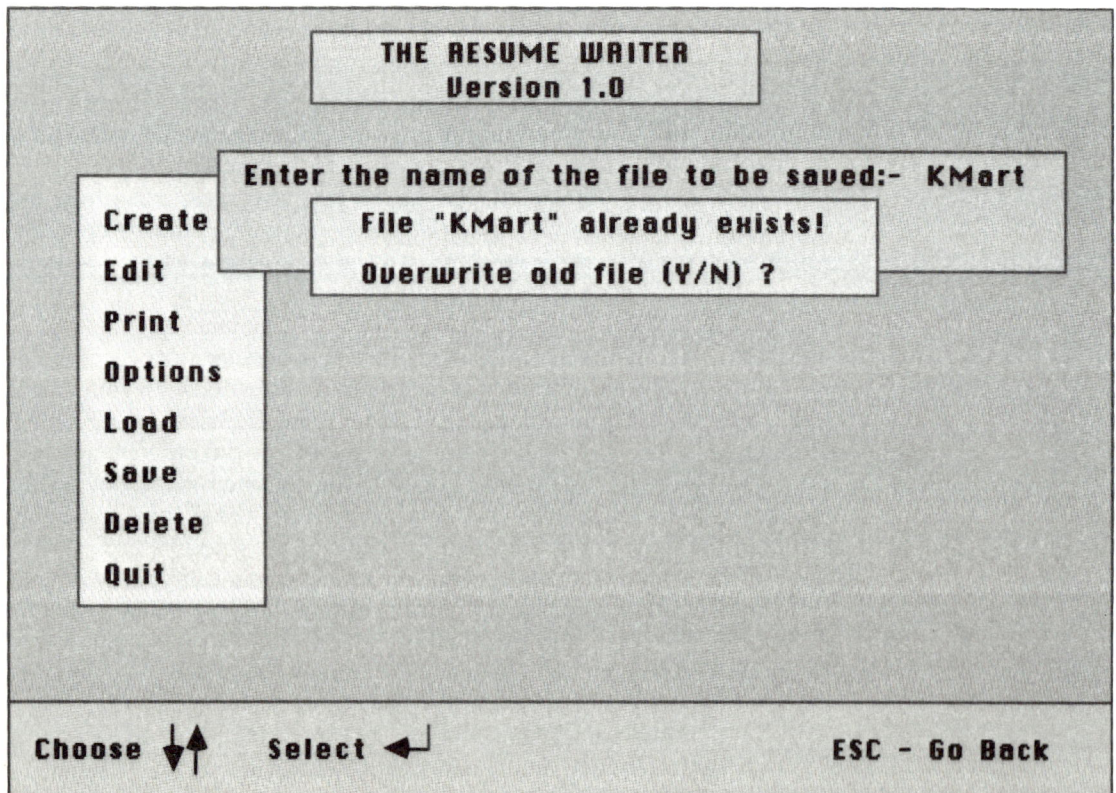

THE RESUME WRITER
Version 1.0

Enter the name of the file to be saved:- KMart

Create
Edit
Print
Options
Load
Save
Delete
Quit

File "KMart" already exists!
Overwrite old file (Y/N) ?

Choose ↓↑   Select ↵   ESC - Go Back

Figure 10-5 Warning of overwriting an existing resume.

3. THE RESUME WRITER will automatically include the extension **.RWF** on the end of any name you come up with, so don't be surprised when you see this tagged on to the end of the name of the files when you look at the listing of your files on your disk.

Something else you should bear in mind is that the name you give a resume file will help you identify it when you subsequently want to load or retrieve the file to make a copy of it on paper or to make changes to it. In other words, when you have, say, half a dozen different versions of your resume on disk, you may start to lose track of which one is which.

Choosing a good name for each of your resume files will make it easy to distinguish one version of your resume from another.

So always choose a name that relates directly to the target audience for that particular version of your resume. It might be a company name, or the name of a specific type of job. Poor names would be a series of names such as Resume1, Resume2, Resume3, etc., because they don't tell you anything about the *content* of each file.

Here are some examples of appropriate names:

Andersen

IBM1989

KMart

Banking

etc.

Safely stowed on THE RESUME WRITER diskette, your resume may be retrieved any time you want to make a new copy of it on the printer, or any time you want to update it by making changes of any kind. This you will do by selecting the **Load** option from the **Main Menu**, which you will learn about in section 10-4.

10.3 MAKING A BACKUP COPY OF YOUR RESUME ON A DISK OTHER THAN THE RESUME WRITER DISKETTE

Making backups is a very important responsibility in a computerized world. Data saved on magnetic media, like diskettes, can easily be lost, no matter how careful you are in the way you handle the diskette.

Put it this way: *Nobody* who has worked with computer systems can say they have never accidentally lost any of their electronically stored data!

You would not like to have to type in all that resume data again, especially if you have customized and saved several versions of your resume on a diskette which has become damaged.

So get into the habit of making a new backup as a matter of course at the end of every session where you make any changes whatsoever to what you have on THE RESUME WRITER diskette.

This will take up no more than perhaps one or two minutes of your time. But if Murphy[1] strikes, and you can bet your bottom dollar he will, you will find yourself spending *hours* of time to recover from your loss.

---

[1] Murphy is the Irish gentleman who is reputed to have said: "If anything can go wrong, it will!"

Actually, there is a corollary to Murphy's law (Poole's corollary) which says: If you are ultra cautious in a computerized environment, Murphy will probably leave you alone. After all, why should he wait around for you to make a mistake when there are plenty of other suckers who are carelessly neglecting to take all due precautions about backup and the like?

This section on backup is of particular interest if you are using a floppy disk drive for THE RESUME WRITER. (If you are using a hard disk drive for your resume writing, you will make backup copies of your resume files to a floppy disk by using the **Copy** command in MS-DOS.)

When you save your resume on disk, you may want to direct it to a diskette other than THE RESUME WRITER diskette. You will, of course, choose the **Save** option from the **Main Menu** in order to do this. Then, before you name the file you are about to save, simply replace THE RESUME WRITER diskette with one of your own formatted diskettes. In response to the prompt for the name of the file, you will type in a suitable name as described above, and press the RETURN key. The system will then go ahead and save the resume on your diskette. This is in fact how you would make backup copies of your resumes.

For example, supposing you wanted to store a file called **Kmart** on a diskette other than THE RESUME WRITER diskette, you would remove THE RESUME WRITER diskette, put your data diskette in the same drive, then simply type the name: **Kmart** in response to the prompt on the screen, followed by RETURN.

When you are done making the backup copy or copies, you should replace your backup diskette with THE RESUME WRITER diskette if you have further resume writing work to do.

10.4   LOADING YOUR RESUME FILE FROM THE RESUME WRITER DISKETTE

You may recall from Section 10.1 that when you run THE RESUME WRITER any time after the first time, the system will automatically load into working memory a default version of your resume from the file called **RESUME.DAT.** This version will always be the one you were last working on. It is also the one that the system will assume is the version that you want to work with now (either to Print, Edit, Layout, Save with its own name, or all of the aforementioned).

In order to load a version other than this default version of your resume from THE RESUME WRITER diskette you must know the name of the file in which that version is stored. Since it is unlikely that you can remember all the different names after a while, it will be useful to have the system list all the names on the screen so you can select the one you want.

10.4.1   VIEWING A LIST OF THE FILES YOU HAVE ON YOUR RESUME WRITER DISKETTE

To do this, you would choose the **Load** option from the **Main Menu** (Fig. 10-6). THE RESUME WRITER will present a window in which will be listed all the resume files that are currently stored on the diskette (Fig. 10-7).

You will use the arrow keys to move through the list of files and select the one that you want to work with by pressing the Return (or Select) key. This file will then be loaded into working memory (Fig. 10-8). Of course, if there are no files on disk the system will warn you of this (Fig. 10-9).

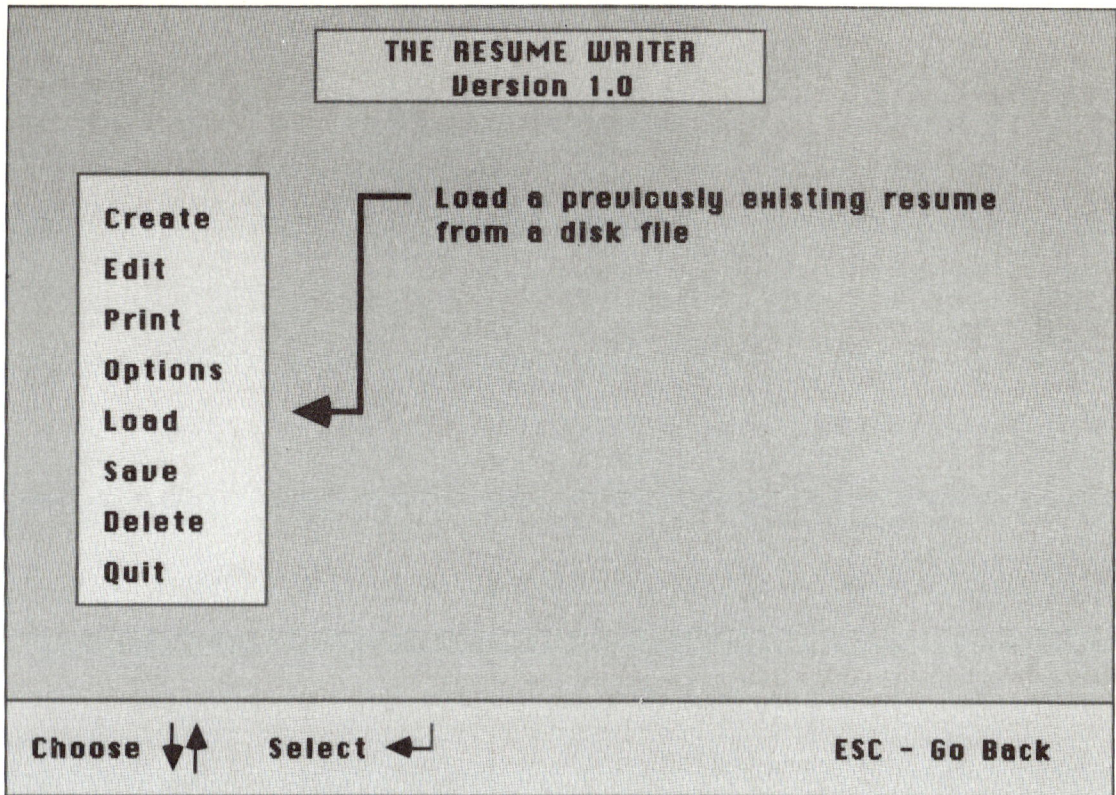

Figure 10-6   The load option from the main menu.

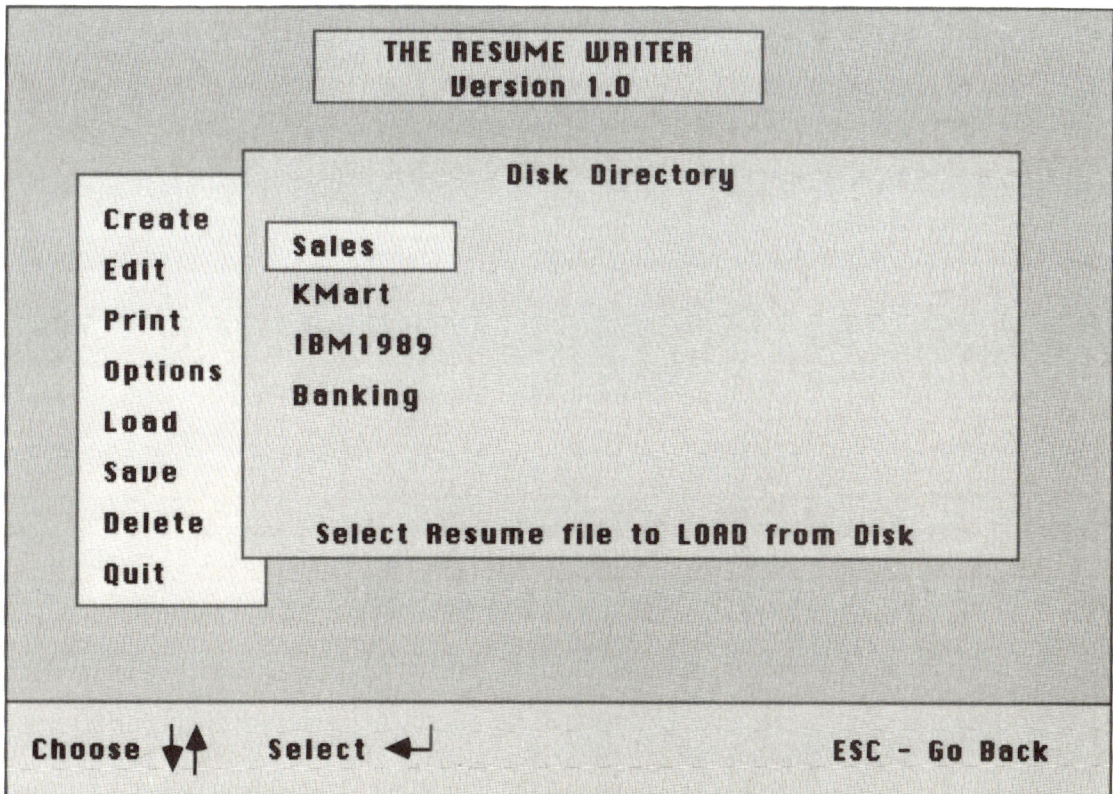

Figure 10-7   Directory of files on disk.

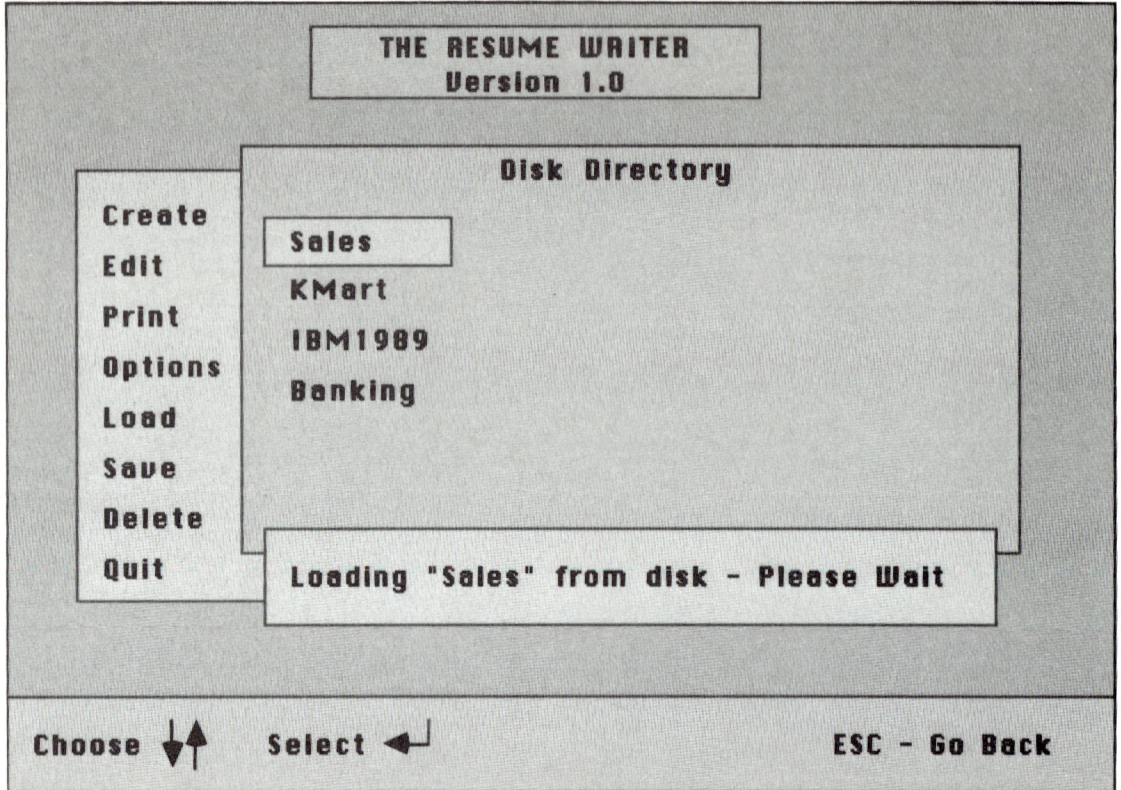

Figure 10-8   Loading a file from the diskette.

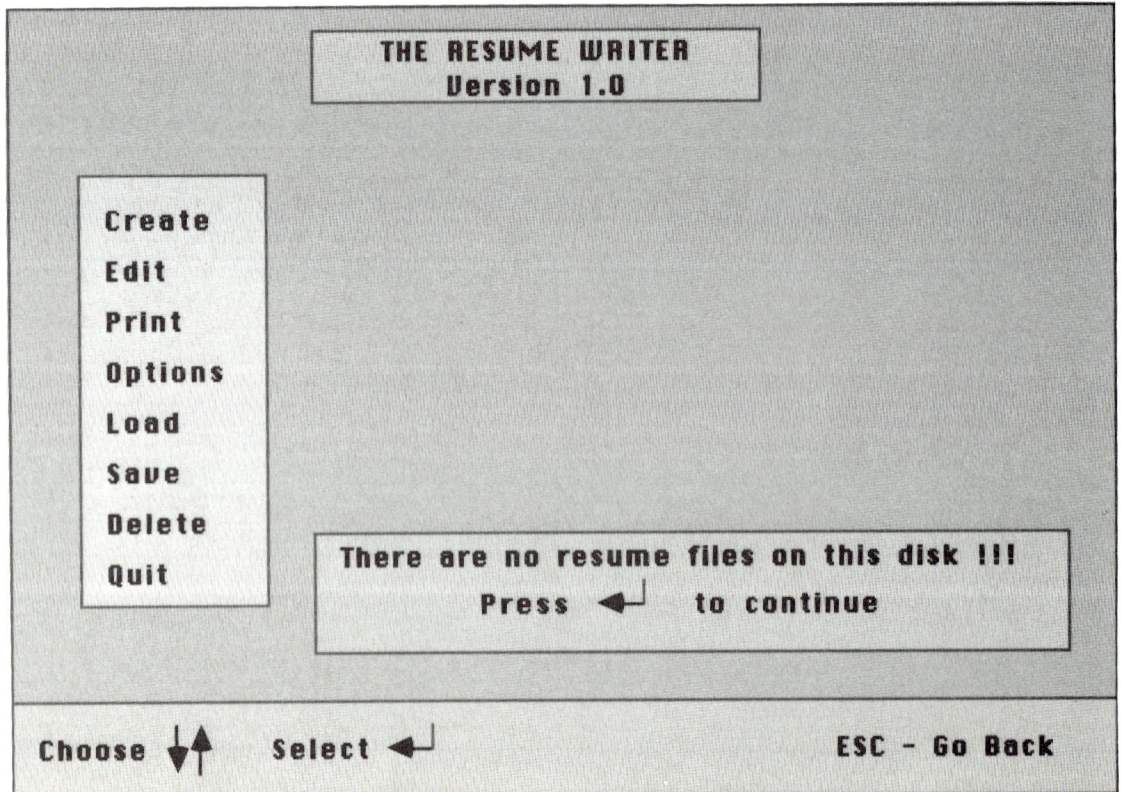

Figure 10-9   Warning that the disk is empty.

10.5 DELETING FILES FROM YOUR DISKS

This is a simple operation. You will select the **Delete** option from the **Main Menu** (Fig. 10-10). The system will then present a list of all the files that you have currently saved on THE RESUME WRITER disk and ask you to select the particular file that you want to delete (Fig. 10-11).

Deleting a file is a significant operation. You should think carefully before you do it. Suppose you go ahead and delete, and then discover that, in haste or because you were distracted (usually by someone named Murphy), you deleted the wrong resume file. Unless you have made a backup copy of all your resume files on another disk, the resume you just deleted is gone forever. For this reason THE RESUME WRITER will ask you if you are sure you want to go ahead and delete the file you have selected (Fig. 10-12).

If you change your mind, you may at this point back out by answering **No**. If you answer **Yes**, the system will do your bidding and remove the file from the diskette (Fig. 10-13).

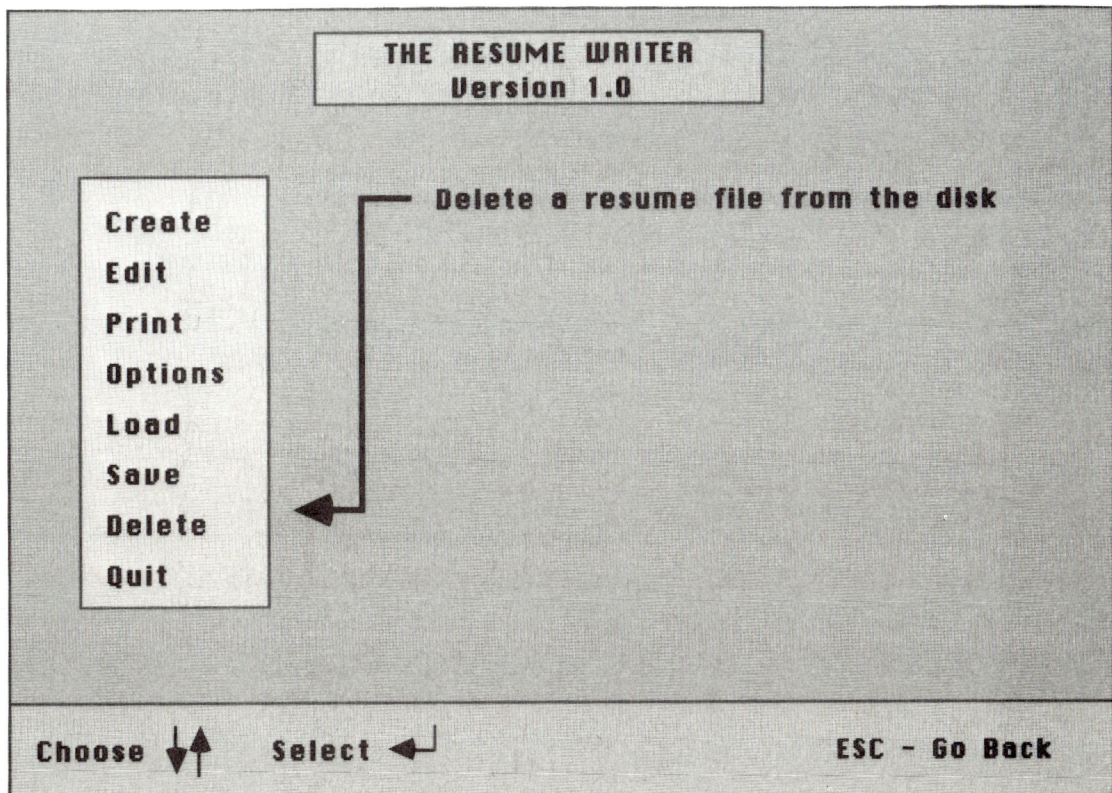

```
                    THE RESUME WRITER
                      Version 1.0


    Create            ┌─ Delete a resume file from the disk
    Edit              │
    Print             │
    Options           │
    Load              │
    Save              │
    Delete    ◄───────┘
    Quit


Choose ↓↑   Select ↵                        ESC - Go Back
```

Figure 10-10   Delete option from the main menu.

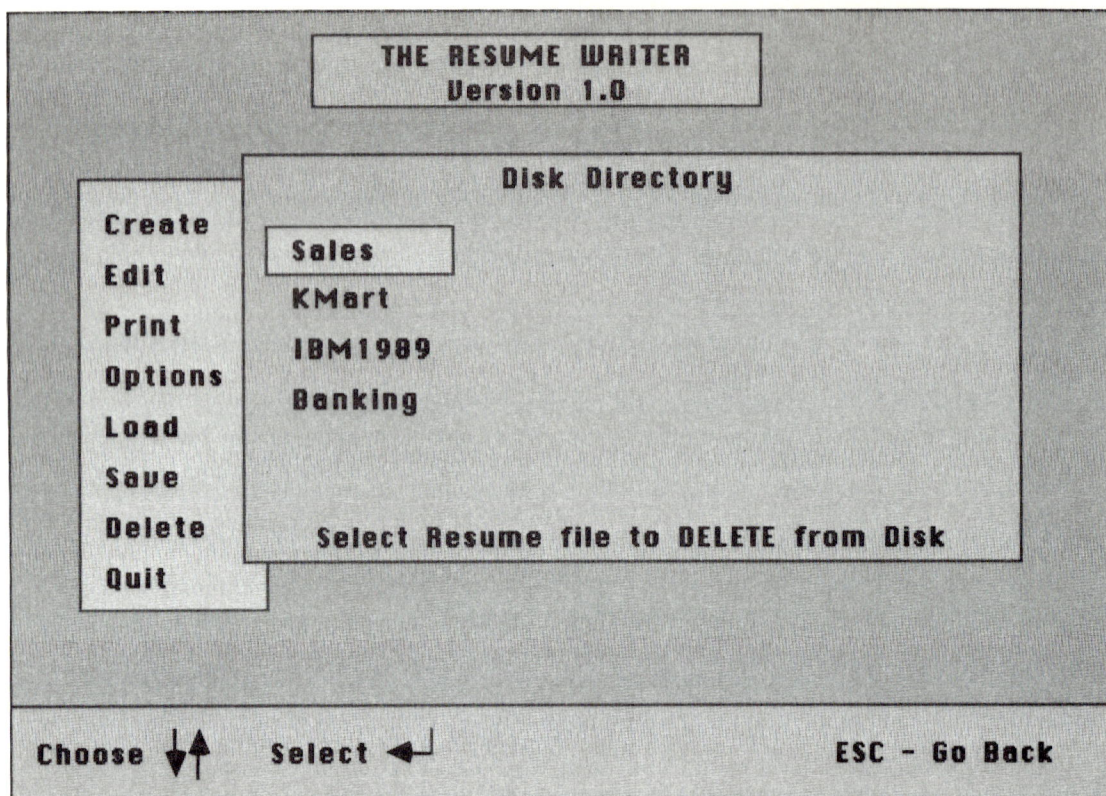

Figure 10-11   Selection of file to delete from the disk.

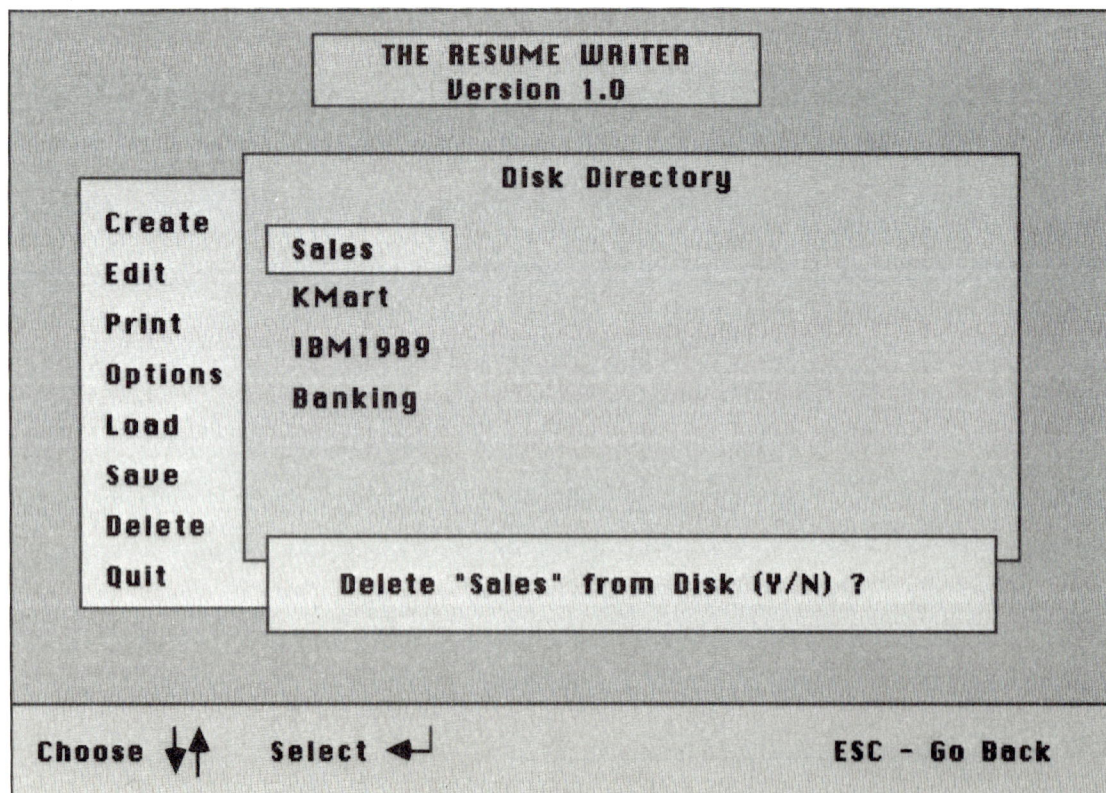

Figure 10-12   Verification prompt to delete a file from the disk.

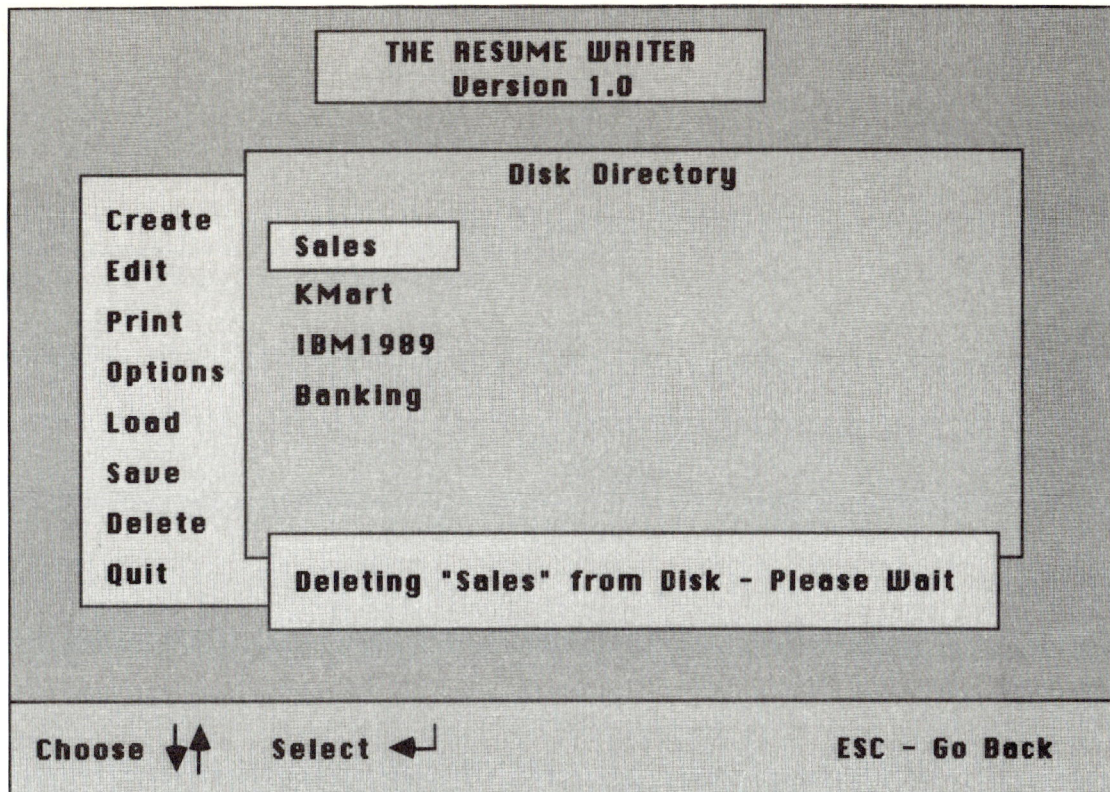

**THE RESUME WRITER
Version 1.0**

Disk Directory

Create

Edit

Print

Options

Load

Save

Delete

Quit

Sales

KMart

IBM1989

Banking

Deleting "Sales" from Disk - Please Wait

Choose ↓↑   Select ↵   ESC - Go Back

Figure 10-13   Deleting the selected file from the diskette.

10.6   MAKING A BACKUP OF THE WORKING COPY OF THE RESUME WRITER DISKETTE

The MASTER copy of THE RESUME WRITER *should not be used to create any resumes at all.* Ideally, it should be the original copy that you purchased along with THE RESUME WRITER text. You should be careful to place a write protect tab over the write protect notch, so that the files on your MASTER disk cannot be accidentally changed or lost in any way. (Appendix A explains in more detail how to handle disks and other items of computer hardware. If you are new to computing, you should read Appendix A before proceeding further.)

Your *working copy* of THE RESUME WRITER, which should be a copy made from the MASTER disk, will have on it the copies of your resume files. It is important to make one or two backup copies of this diskette, especially if you have not taken the file backup option already described in Section 10-3 above. Ideally, you will make backup copies of THE RESUME WRITER diskette at the end of every working session.

Here is the procedure for making a backup copy of a diskette other than the MASTER:

To make a duplicate of a working copy of THE RESUME WRITER you need your computer with one or two floppy disk drives. If you have a hard drive on your system, you will undoubtedly have MS-DOS or PC-DOS already installed, so you can skip direction #1 and direction #2. Also, if you already have THE RESUME WRITER booted, with the

Main Menu on the screen, you can just choose **Quit**, and skip the first two directions.

Follow these directions **CAREFULLY.**

1. Put **MS-DOS** or **PC-DOS (version 2.0 or higher)** in **DRIVE A**.
2. If the computer is *not* already turned on, turn it on and wait for the system to set itself up.

    If, however, the computer is already turned on, reset the system by simultaneously pressing the **CTRL, ALT, DEL** keys, as described in Appendix A.
3. After a few seconds the last item on the computer screen should be the **A:\>** prompt (**C:\>** if you are using a hard disk drive). Assuming this is the case, and that you have *two* floppy drives type

    DISKCOPY A: B:

    and press the **RETURN** key.
4. The system will ask you to put the Source diskette (THE RESUME WRITER diskette) in **DRIVE A**.

    The system will also ask you to put the Target diskette (your backup diskette) in **DRIVE B**.

    Once both diskettes are installed in their respective drives, press any key to start the disk copy process.

    If you have just one floppy drive, type the command

    DISKCOPY A: A:

    and press the RETURN key. Then follow the directions that appear on the screen.
5. The system will now take over, and for the next minute or so will copy all the data from THE RESUME WRITER diskette to your blank backup diskette.
6. When the copy is complete, the system will ask if you want to make another copy. You will answer "**Y**" or "**N**" accordingly.

You should keep at least two working copies of THE RESUME WRITER containing all the versions of your resume.

7. Use a sticky label to identify your diskette as THE RESUME WRITER backup (Backup I, Backup II, etc.).

It is advisable to write on the sticky label *before* you put it on your backup diskettes. However, if you have already attached the labels, be sure to use nothing other than a felt tip pen to identify the disk. Ball point or pencil require extra pressure and might result in damage to the diskette.

8. Keep your backup diskettes current by making backups whenever you use THE RESUME WRITER. Remember, a computer system is only as organized as you are!

Once you have your resume safely saved on disk, you may well subsequently want to make changes to it. In the next chapter you will learn how to edit a resume using THE RESUME WRITER.

Editing Your Resume

LEARNING OBJECTIVES:

In this chapter you will learn how to use THE RESUME WRITER to make changes to your resume both while you are in the process of creating it, and after you have saved it on your disk. You will be able to delete sections, rewrite sections that already exist, as well as add new sections that you originally overlooked:

- ▢ Calling the Edit function from the Main Menu
- ▢ Using the Edit menu
- ▢ Deleting a section of your resume
- ▢ Adding a new section to your resume

It has been demonstrated many times over that computer-assisted writing (using a word processor or THE RESUME WRITER) improves the *quality* of your writing. There is nothing magical about this. Any time you know you can easily correct your mistakes, you will be more than willing to do just that.

Hand-written or typewritten work has a "chiselled in stone" feel to it. Once committed to paper, making changes is either messy, or a nightmare, or both. Word processed work, on the other hand, is like Play Dough—you can mold, massage, and manipulate your writing into whatever shape you want.

Knowing how easy it is to make changes will encourage you to seek advice on wording, phraseology, and layout. So your work becomes a team effort, and you come out the winner every time. Not only is the process of producing your resume a more complete learning experience, but the end product is more likely to be a top quality commercial for your showcase of talents.

11.1   CALLING THE EDIT FUNCTION FROM THE MAIN MENU

Editing a previously created resume is easy enough using THE RESUME WRITER. The first thing you must do is LOAD the version of your resume that you want to edit. So you must select **Load** from the **Main Menu**. When the system presents the list of resume files that you have on disk, highlight the one that you want to edit and press the Return key. The light will show on the disk drive as the system loads your resume into working memory.

Then, in order to enter the Edit function, select **Edit** from the **Main Menu** (Fig. 11-1). The system will immediately present a new screen with a list of all the major sections of the specific resume format that is in working memory (Fig. 11-2). Thus, for a chronological resume, the menu includes all possible sections for that format.

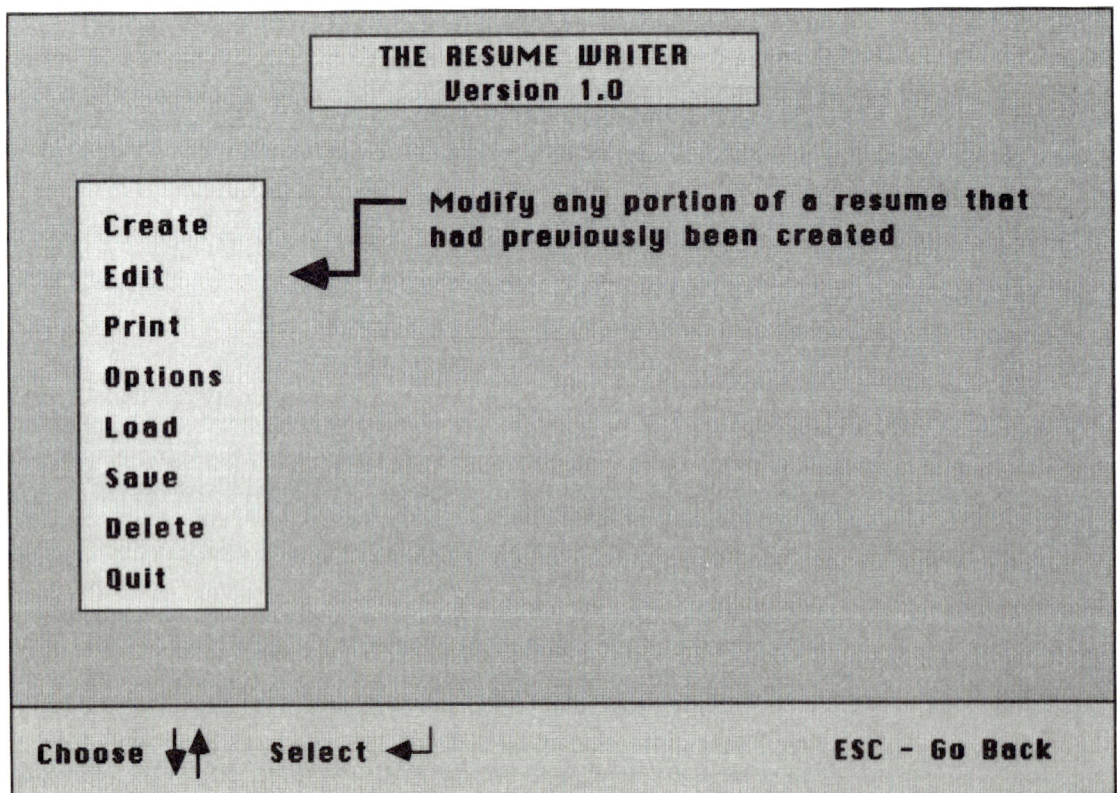

Figure 11-1   Edit option from the main menu.

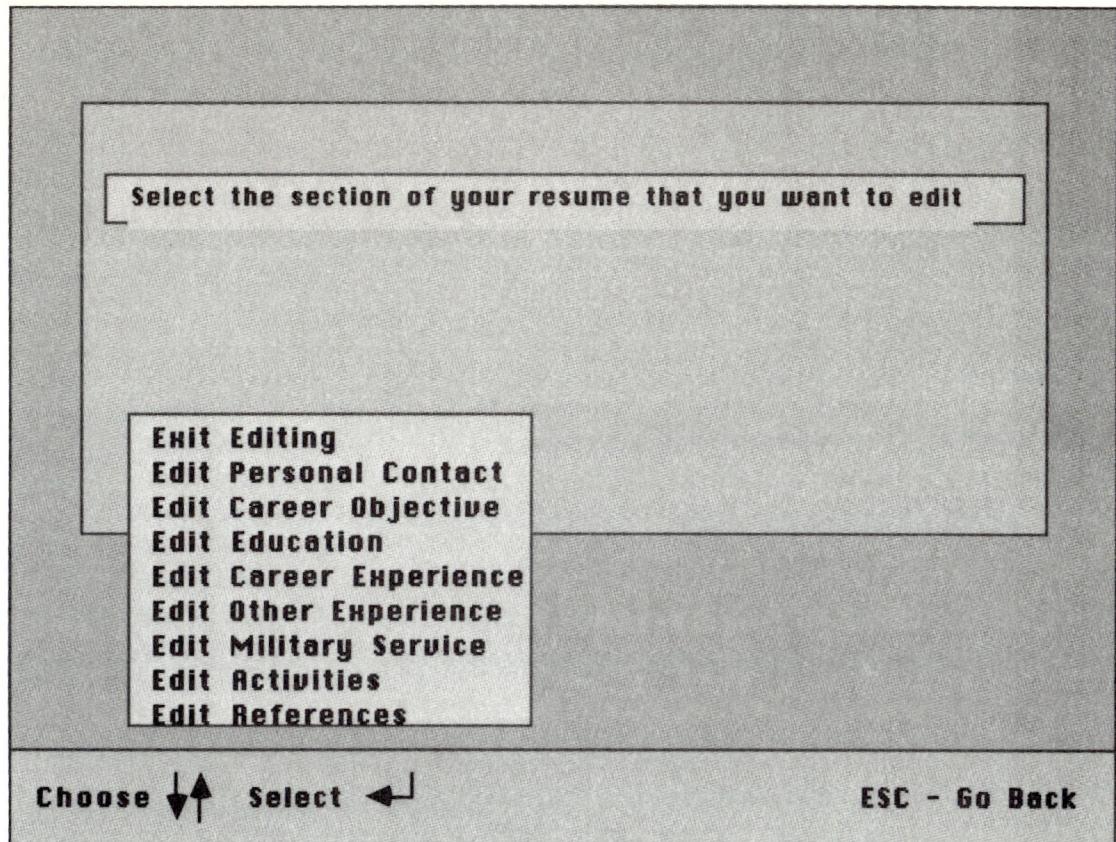

```
┌─────────────────────────────────────────────────────┐
│ Select the section of your resume that you want to edit │
└─────────────────────────────────────────────────────┘



      ┌───────────────────────────────┐
      │  Exit Editing                 │
      │  Edit Personal Contact        │
      │  Edit Career Objective        │
      │  Edit Education               │
      │  Edit Career Experience       │
      │  Edit Other Experience        │
      │  Edit Military Service        │
      │  Edit Activities              │
      │  Edit References              │
      └───────────────────────────────┘

  Choose ↓↑   Select ←                    ESC - Go Back
```

Figure 11-2 Sample edit menu screen.

11.2 USING THE EDIT MENU

If you look at the Edit menu as illustrated in Fig. 11-2, you will notice that it lists only the main sections of the resume, such as Personal Contact, etc. In order to edit a specific item in your resume you will need to know which of these main sections it appears in, and then select that section. For example, your name is clearly part of the Personal Contact section, as indeed would be your address and telephone number.

If this is not obvious to you, all you have to do is select each main section in turn, and another menu will pop up on the screen itemizing the contents of that section. Fig. 11-3, for example, shows the menu that will be presented on the screen if you select the Personal Contact section. As you can see, the menu asks you to select again, this time to either edit the one address that you already have in the resume, or to add a second address.

If you already had two addresses included in your resume, you would see a slightly different menu (Fig. 11-4). Now you are asked to choose to edit one or the other of the two addresses.

Needless to say, you always have the option to do nothing, and immediately exit the section. Thus, you can use the menus to browse through the various sections to see exactly what changes you want to make where.

You are never committed to making a change just because you have chosen to edit your resume.

Suppose you select to edit one of the addresses. THE RESUME WRITER will present the last level edit menu (Fig. 11-5) which lists the specific data items

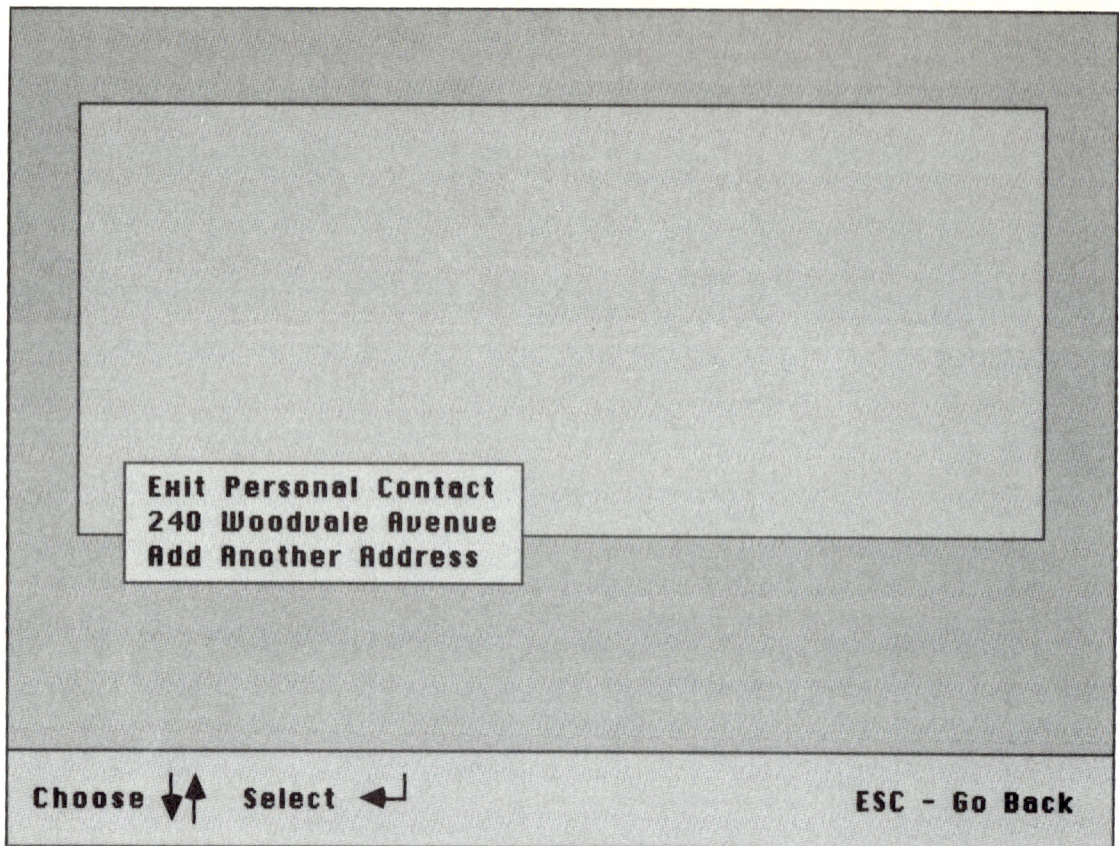

```
Exit Personal Contact
240 Woodvale Avenue
Add Another Address
```

Choose ↓↑ Select ◄┘   ESC - Go Back

Figure 11-3   Personal contact edit menu for one address.

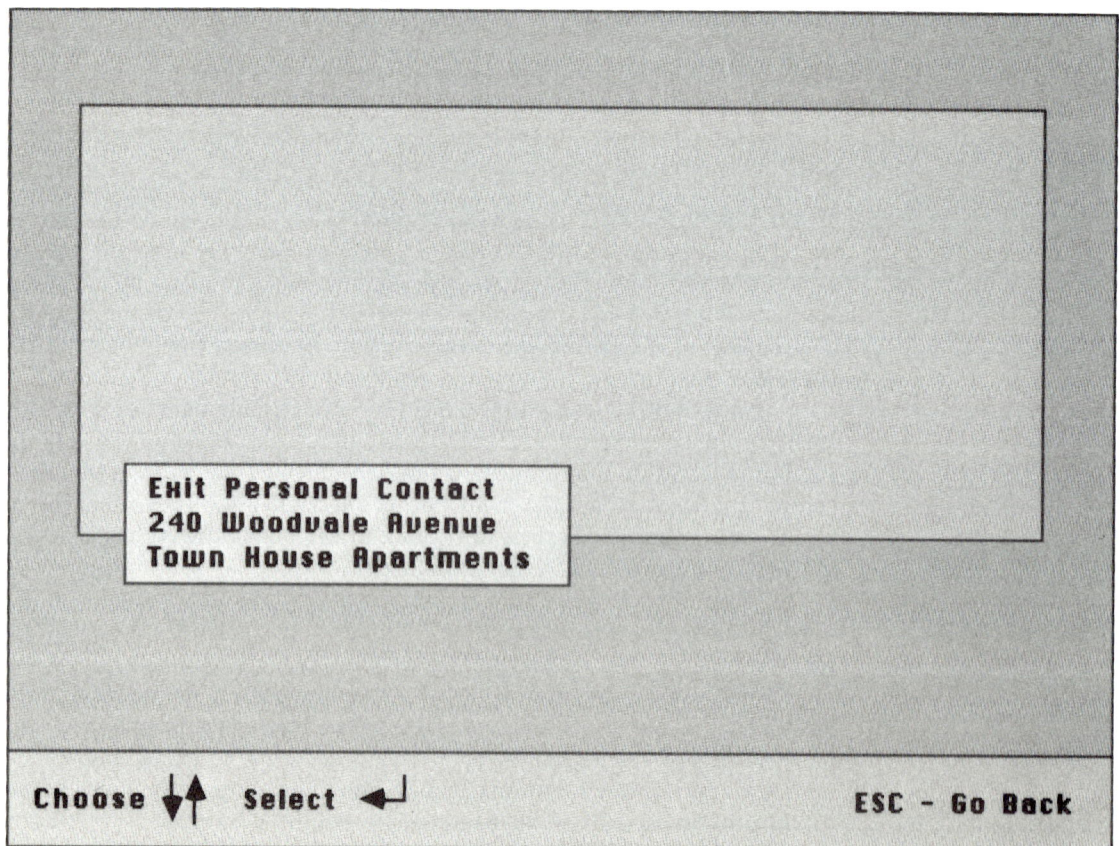

```
Exit Personal Contact
240 Woodvale Avenue
Town House Apartments
```

Choose ↓↑ Select ◄┘   ESC - Go Back

Figure 11-4   Personal contact edit menu for two addresses.

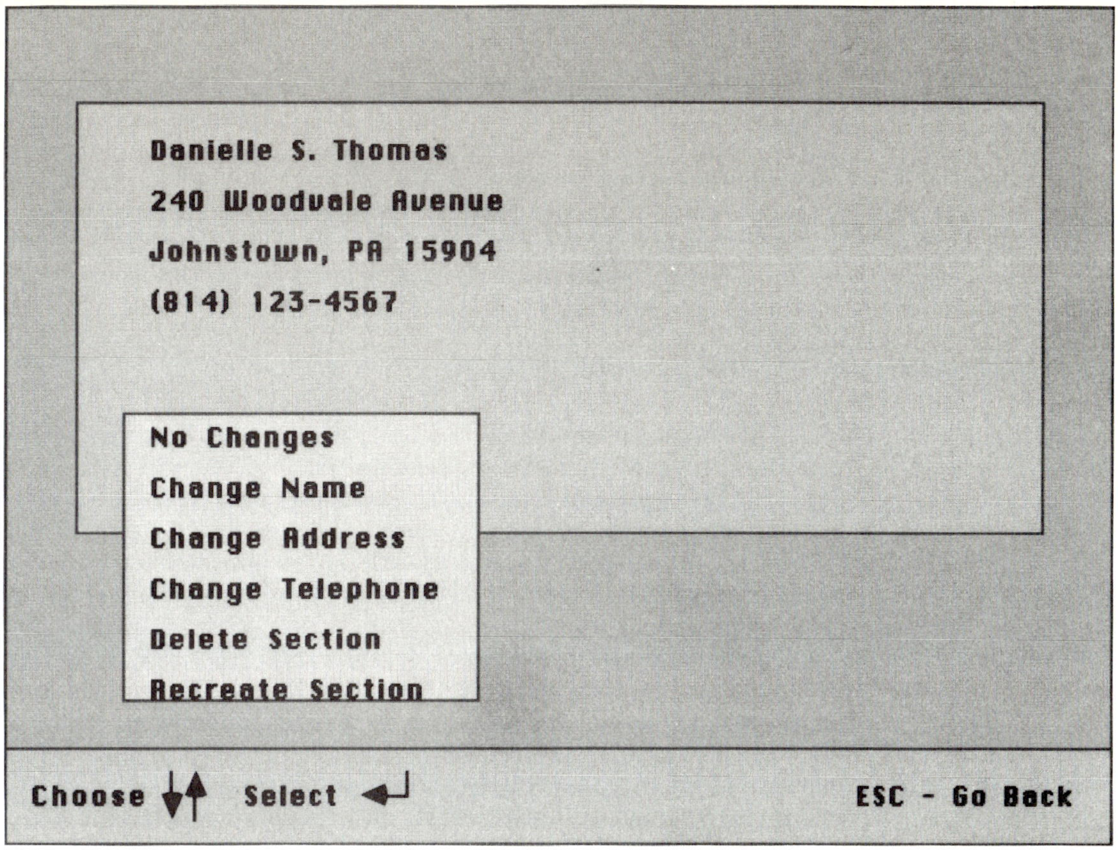

Figure 11-5   Base level edit menu for personal contact.

you may select to change in the name and address. On the same screen, the system displays the data you previously entered so that you can visually check before opting to go ahead and make changes.

Even now, supposing you select to change the address, the system will present the original data entry screen which captured your address in the first place. But this time all the data will be filled in. The cursor will be waiting at the end of the first line of your address. If all you wanted to change was, say, a misspelling of the city, you would press the Return key until the cursor is at the end of the city name, backspace as far over the name as you need to go to correct the error, and then retype it. Finally, you would press the Return key until you saw the customary prompt:

Is the above information correct   Y/N   ?

If you answer Yes, you will be taken back to the edit menu for the Personal Contact section. Exiting the Personal Contact menu will take you back to the top level Edit menu, from where you can exit to the Main Menu.

After creating a first version of your resume on the diskette, you should take some time to browse through these edit menus so as to familiarize yourself with the various paths you can take through them. None of the Edit menus has more than three levels, and each menu is well sign-posted, so there is no danger of your getting lost in them.

11.3   DELETING AND REPLACING A SECTION OF YOUR RESUME

As an alternative to changing an item here and there, it is always possible to delete an entire section of your resume. Having deleted it, you may choose either to leave out the data or reenter it. Just select from the top level Edit menu the section that you want to edit in this way. Then, at the next level you will have the option to simply delete, or delete and replace (recreate).

The menu illustrated in Fig. 11-5 is a typical example of where you have both the Delete and Recreate options included among the choices you can make.

11.4   ADDING A NEW SECTION TO YOUR RESUME

As indicated at the end of Section 11.1, the top level Edit menu is sensitive to the type of resume you have in working memory. You will therefore be able to add sections to your resume which you omitted on a first draft.

When it comes down to it, you have the capability, using THE RESUME WRITER, to change as much or as little as you want whenever you want. Without such flexibility it would be lacking in its usefulness to you as a tool in the job search.

It must be said again, however, that THE RESUME WRITER will not write the resume for you, nor will it edit it for you. As stressed in PART I of this book, the responsibility is yours to write appropriate material, and to proofread everything you do. It is also essential to have someone else review what you have prepared. Objective reviewers are much more likely to find your errors than you are yourself. But if you take the time to do a thorough, careful job, you will find THE RESUME WRITER a valuable tool in putting together an effective resume.

The last step in the preparation of any resume, and certainly as important as any other step, is that of putting it on paper. The process of printing your resume will be discussed in the next chapter.

chapter 12

Printing Your Resume

LEARNING OBJECTIVES:

Once you have the data for your resume collected and saved in a file on disk, you are ready to send it to the printer. In the first part of this chapter you will learn to use the various functions that enable you to:

- □ set up THE RESUME WRITER so that it can interact with your printer
- □ test the printer to make sure that the printer controls on your printer are understood by THE RESUME WRITER
- □ establish the layout that you would like for your resume on paper

The second part of this chapter will explain how to send your resume to the printer once you have prepared it for printing. If you are already familiar with your computer system, much of this section will be unnecessary reading. If, however, you are using the computer for the first time, say at your school or place of business, you will find useful hints in this chapter to help you to:

- □ prepare the printer for printing
  - □ select the number of copies you require
  - □ align the paper correctly in the printer
- □ send the resume to the printer

12.1 SETTING UP THE RESUME WRITER SO THAT IT CAN INTERACT WITH YOUR PRINTER

It is possible that your printer is compatible with the printer codes that have been set up as the default text layout settings for THE RESUME WRITER (EPSON 85 or EPSON 185). If this is so, you need do nothing in the way of setting up THE RESUME WRITER for your printer since this has already been done for you.

In order to verify whether or not your printer has the default settings, you should test the printer. Section 12.2 shows you how to do this.

If, when you send your resume to the printer, the output looks strange in any way, this will probably be because THE RESUME WRITER does not recognize the printer codes for layout specifications such as underlining, centering, italics, and so on.

In this case, you will need to tell THE RESUME WRITER what kind of printer you have attached to your system. This is done by selecting **Options** from the **Main Menu** (Fig. 12-1).

Unfortunately, there are many different brands of printers in the IBM world, and some of them have a unique way of handling commands that layout the data on the printed page. This section of Chapter Twelve is only relevant the first time you use THE RESUME WRITER with a particular computer system. You will need to check that THE RESUME WRITER is set up to work with the printer attached to the system you are using. As long as you use the same system,

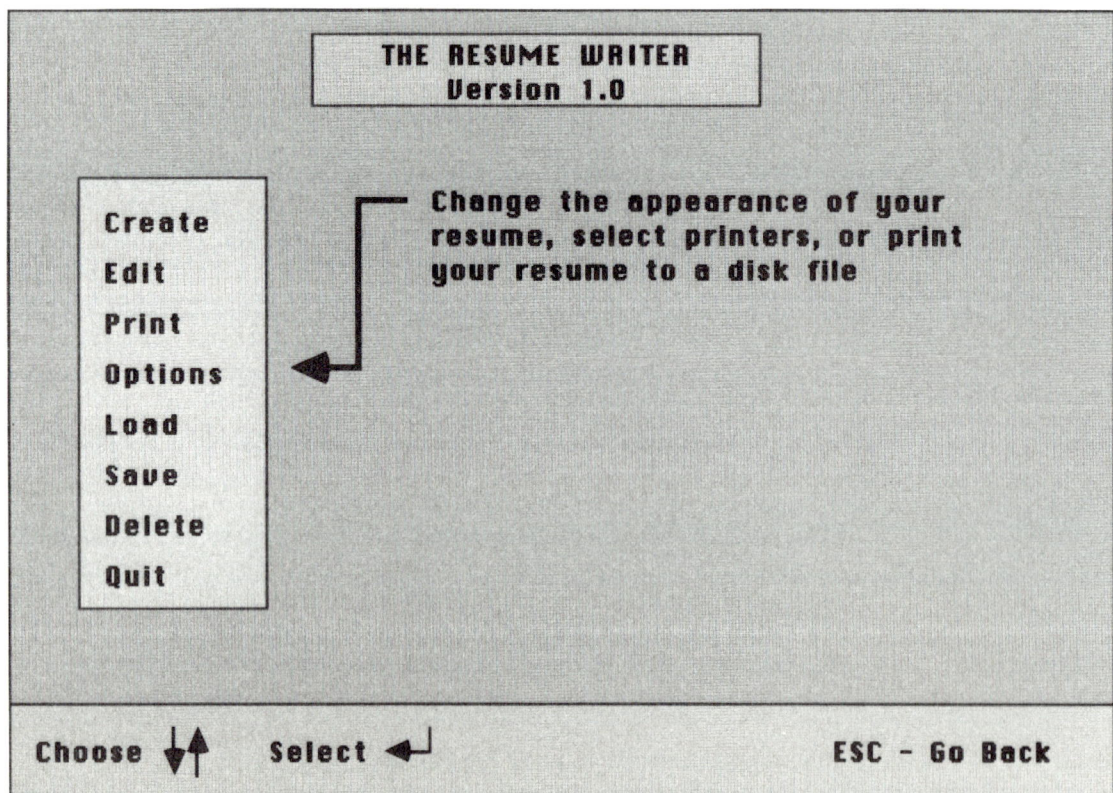

Figure 12-1 Options selection from the main menu.

you need only do this once. But if you move to a system that has a different kind of printer attached to it, you may have to go through the **Select Printer** function again.

Selecting **Options** from the **Main Menu** will cause a second menu to pop up on the screen (Fig. 12-2). The first item in this menu allows you to select from a list of printers that are compatible with THE RESUME WRITER (Fig. 12-3).

This list of printers is not exhaustive, but it covers many of the popular printers used at the present time. If your type of printer does not show up in the list, it is very possible that one of the other printers listed will use the same codes as yours. So you might need to experiment the first time until you are happy with the output that is produced by your printer. Select each printer in turn, then, after accepting the changed printer, **ESC** back to the Options Menu (Fig. 12-2) and select **Test Printer**. The system will show you how the printer will handle your resume output with the new printer codes you just selected.

In the unlikely event that, after testing them all, none of the listed printers is compatible with your own you have at least three options:

1. If you have access (at a school or college you attend, or at your place of work) to another IBM compatible computer system that uses one of the printers listed in THE RESUME WRITER you might print out your resume there.
2. Most printing businesses today have computerized operations and may be able to print your resume for you.

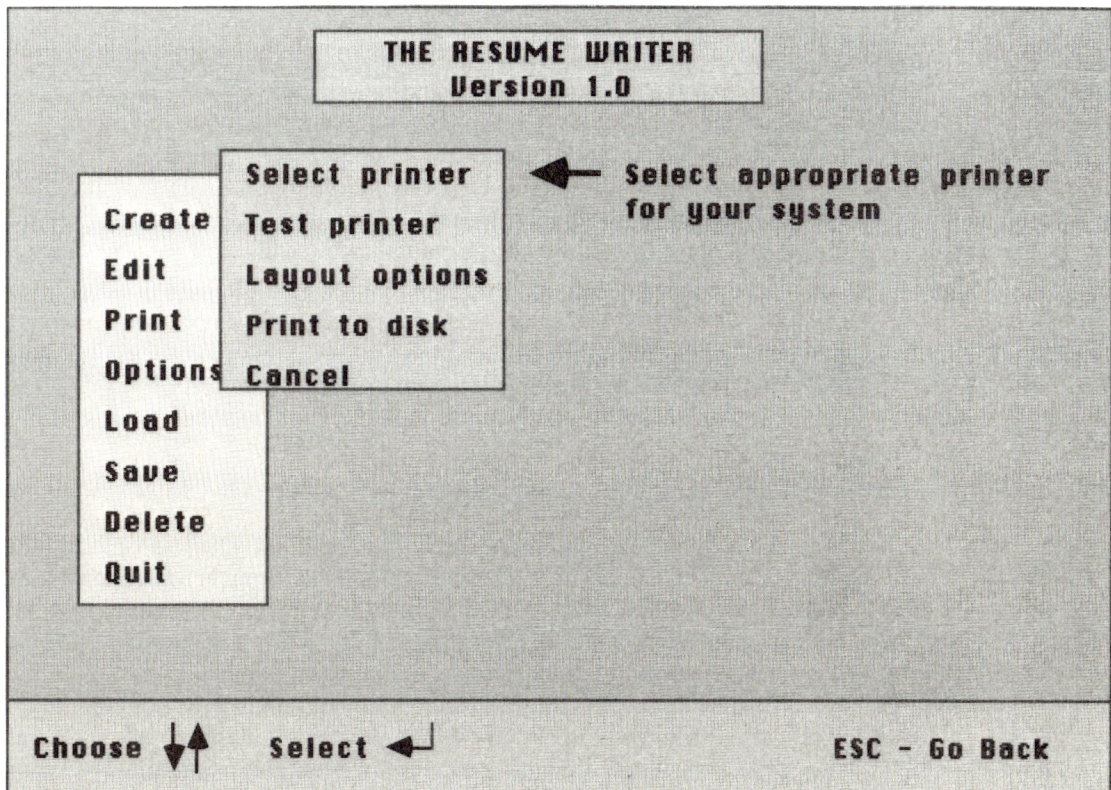

```
                   THE RESUME WRITER
                     Version 1.0

             Select printer    ◄─── Select appropriate printer
   Create   Test printer             for your system
   Edit     Layout options
   Print    Print to disk
   Options  Cancel
   Load
   Save
   Delete
   Quit


Choose ↓↑    Select ↵                        ESC - Go Back
```

Figure 12-2   Select printer option from options menu.

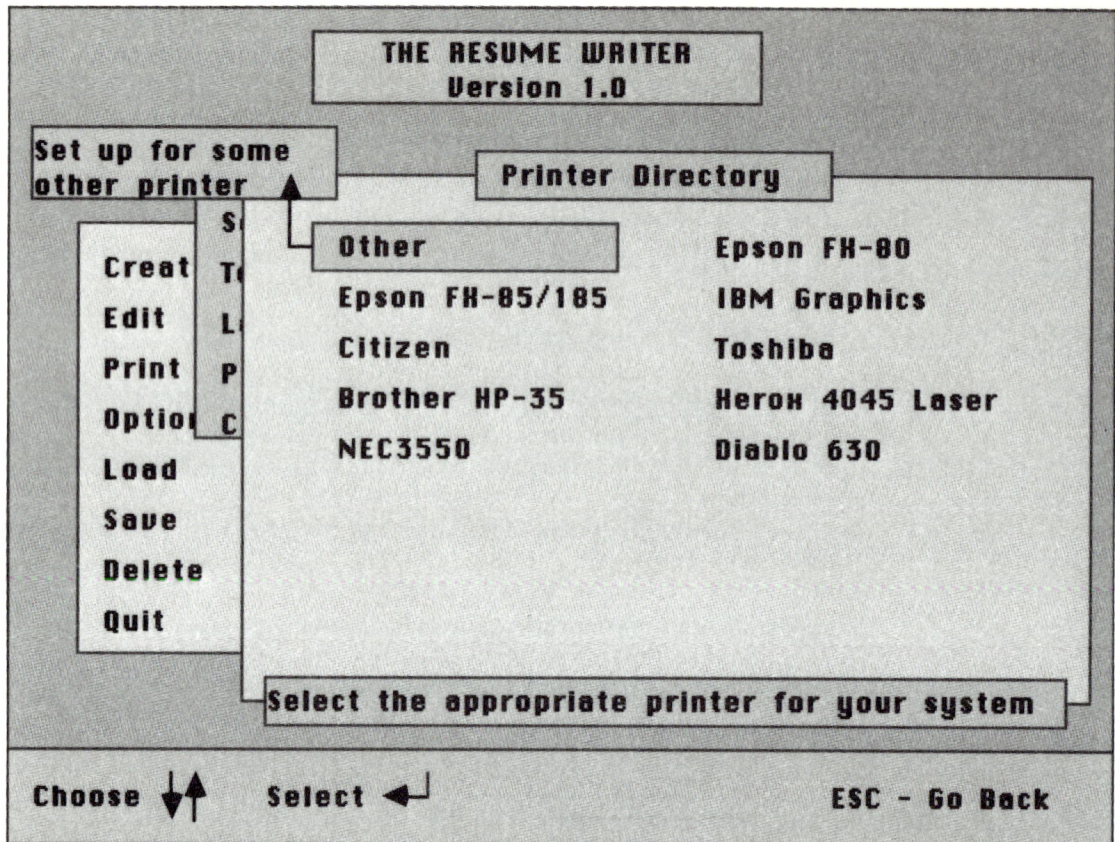

Figure 12-3   Printer directory.

3. If you consider yourself a Power User, and are not fazed by some of the technical aspects of your computer system, you can customize THE RESUME WRITER to work with the unique printer codes that apply to your machine. To do this you would select "Other" as your printer choice. THE RESUME WRITER will then step you through the process of supplying the appropriate codes, and testing them with your printer. The appropriate codes may be found in the Reference Manual supplied with your printer when you originally purchased it.

12.2   TESTING YOUR PRINTER

Fig. 12-4 illustrates the menu selection from the **Options** menu which allows you to test your printer. Selecting the Test Printer option will cause THE RESUME WRITER to print a page of text (Fig. 12-5) which will exercise all the text layout codes that have been set up in the software, either by default, or because you selected them for your particular printer. If all is well, you should be able to examine the page produced by the Test Printer option and verify that the italics code does indeed print in italics, the underline code does indeed cause the printer to underline, and so forth. Any inconsistencies will suggest that the printer settings are not appropriate, and that you should follow the guidelines in Section 12.1 of this chapter to rectify the situation.

```
                    ┌─────────────────────────┐
                    │   THE RESUME WRITER     │
                    │      Version 1.0        │
                    └─────────────────────────┘


         ┌──────────────────────────┐
         │  Select printer          │    ┌─Run a test program that will
  Creat  │  Test printer            │◄───┘ print the available font styles
  Edit   │  Layout options          │      supported by your printer
  Print  │  Print to disk           │
  Option │  Cancel                  │
  Load   └──────────────────────────┘
  Save
  Delete
  Quit


  Choose ↓↑    Select ◄┘                        ESC - Go Back
```

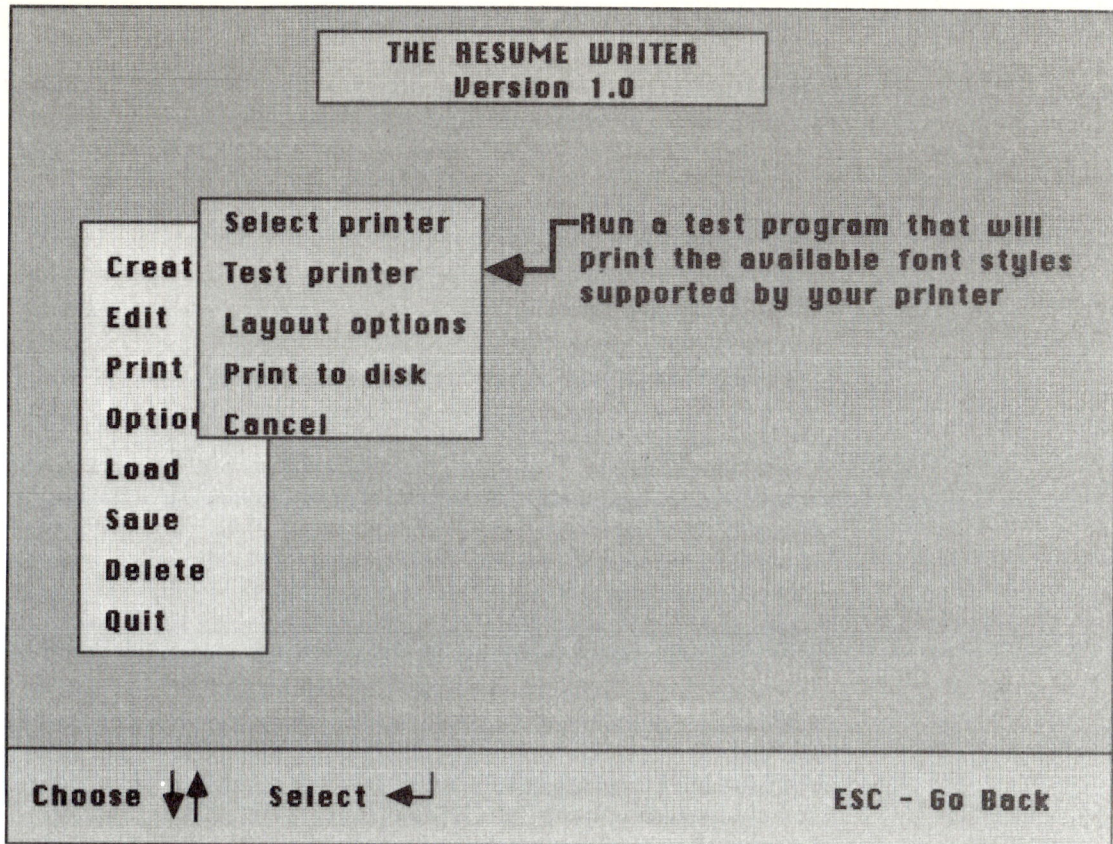

Figure 12-4 Test printer option from options menu.

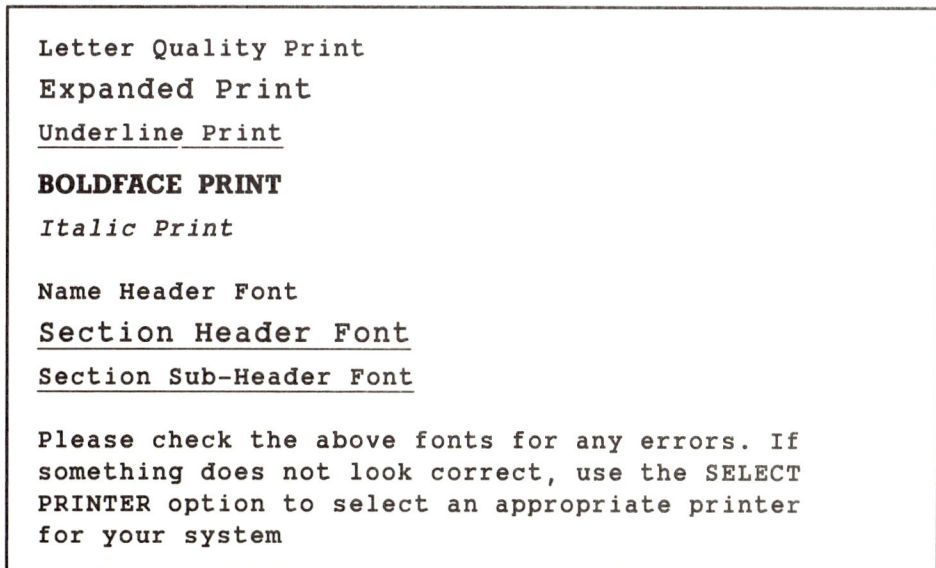

```
┌────────────────────────────────────────────────┐
│                                                  │
│  Letter Quality Print                            │
│  Expanded Print                                  │
│  Underline Print                                 │
│                                                  │
│  BOLDFACE PRINT                                  │
│  Italic Print                                    │
│                                                  │
│  Name Header Font                                │
│  Section Header Font                             │
│  Section Sub-Header Font                         │
│                                                  │
│  Please check the above fonts for any errors. If │
│  something does not look correct, use the SELECT │
│  PRINTER option to select an appropriate printer │
│  for your system                                 │
│                                                  │
└────────────────────────────────────────────────┘
```

Figure 12-5 Display of printer typefaces and fonts.

12.3 ESTABLISHING THE LAYOUT OF YOUR RESUME ON PAPER

There are innumerable ways of laying out a resume on paper. In practice, however, the variety is limited by certain obvious criteria:

- the resume should use white space liberally so that it does not look too cluttered;
- the resume should look tidy;
- the resume should allow the reader's eyes to easily move from section to section;
- the resume should highlight significant features.

THE RESUME WRITER does not allow you complete freedom, *from within the program,* about the layout of your resume. Nonetheless, it gives you sufficient flexibility to produce a final product which, while fulfilling the criteria outlined above, also allows you to incorporate individual preferences. The problem with complete freedom is that you may not know what *is* the best layout to choose. With THE RESUME WRITER you can relax because whichever layout you choose, the final product will end up looking very presentable indeed.

If you are an experienced writer, or if your skills in the creative arts need emphasizing through your resume, you will probably want to take advantage of the Power User capability of THE RESUME WRITER. In this case you should read Chapter Thirteen, which explains what you need to do to integrate the resume that you produce using THE RESUME WRITER with the word processor of your choice.

Laying out your resume will take some experimentation on your part. You might begin by allowing the system to print your resume using the default layout settings that are built into the program. To do this follow the directions as explained in the next section (Section 12.4).

Alternatively, if you select **Layout Options** from the **Options Menu** (Fig. 12-6) you will be presented with a window which contains a listing of possible layout settings that you can choose for different parts of your resume (Fig. 12-7). Let's look at them one by one.

Name Header: For this part of your resume you have the option to print your name **Expanded** as well as underlined and/or **bold face**. It is generally not recommended that your name be italicized. However, if you insist on this feature you can always take advantage of the Power User option explained in Chapter Thirteen.

Where you have only one address you can also opt to print the Name Header section, including the address, centered at the top of each page. If you have two addresses, they will be printed on the left and right, as one might expect, but your name may still be either centered or left justified.

Section Headers: Section headers should stand out, so THE RESUME WRITER displays them on a line by themselves. Once again, however, you may individualize the final product by **bold face**, underlining, or **expand**ing them. You can also of course, mix the options by using **bold face along with underlining**, for example. The golden rule is

```
+------------------------------------------------------------------+
|                   THE RESUME WRITER                              |
|                     Version 1.0                                 |
|                                                                  |
|         +----------------------+                                 |
|         | Select printer       |    Change the appearance of     |
|  Creat  | Test printer         |    your printed resume          |
|  Edit   | Layout options    <--+                                 |
|  Print  | Print to disk        |                                 |
|  Optiol | Cancel               |                                 |
|  Load   +----------------------+                                 |
|  Save                                                            |
|  Delete                                                          |
|  Quit                                                            |
|                                                                  |
|  Choose  ↓↑    Select  ↵              ESC - Go Back              |
+------------------------------------------------------------------+
```

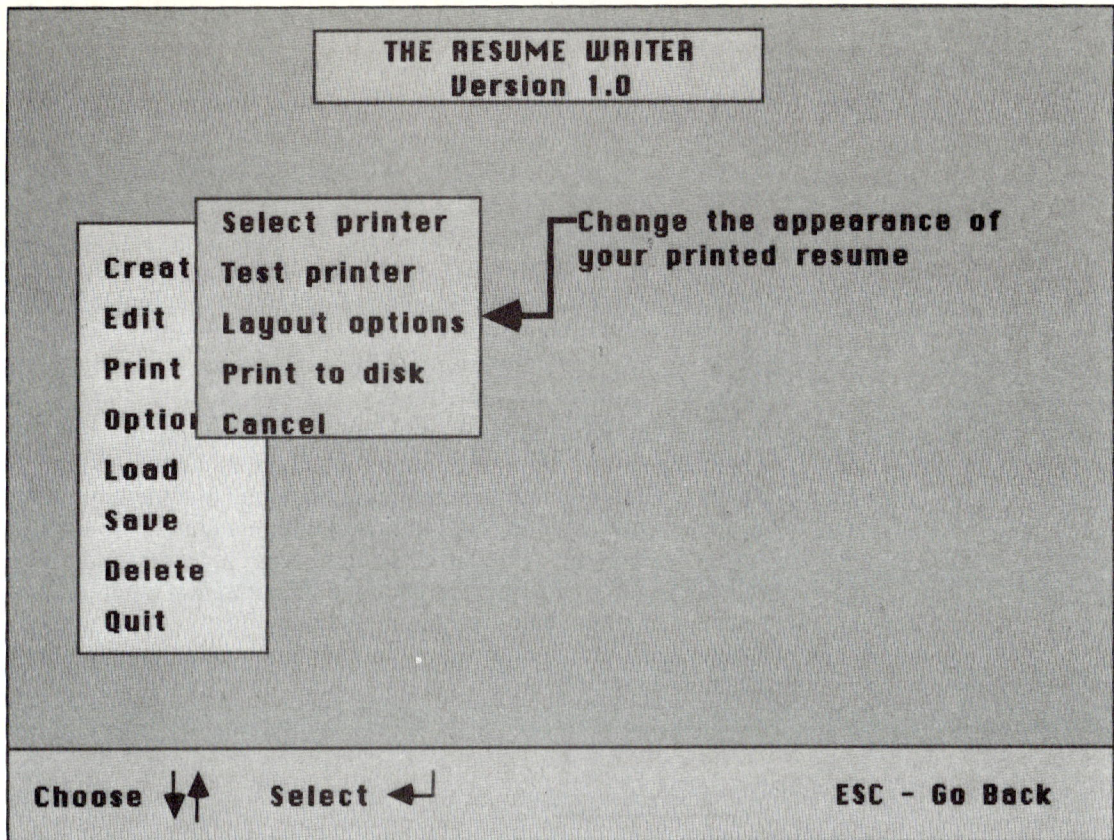

Figure 12-6   Layout options from the options menu.

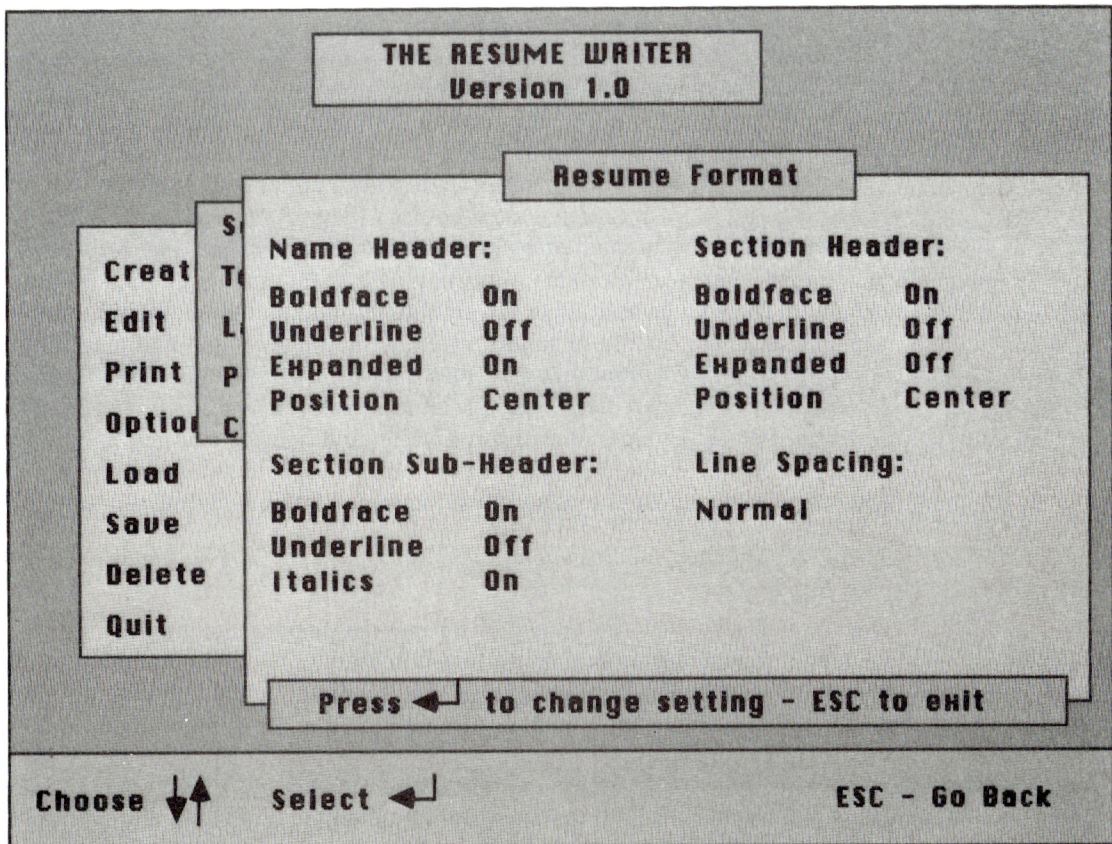

```
+------------------------------------------------------------------+
|                   THE RESUME WRITER                              |
|                     Version 1.0                                 |
|                                                                  |
|              +----------------------------------------+          |
|              |           Resume Format                |          |
|         S    |                                        |          |
|  Creat  T    | Name Header:        Section Header:     |          |
|  Edit   L    |                                        |          |
|  Print  P    | Boldface    On      Boldface    On     |          |
|  Optiol C    | Underline   Off     Underline   Off    |          |
|  Load        | Expanded    On      Expanded    Off    |          |
|  Save        | Position    Center  Position    Center |          |
|  Delete      |                                        |          |
|  Quit        | Section Sub-Header: Line Spacing:       |          |
|              |                                        |          |
|              | Boldface    On      Normal             |          |
|              | Underline   Off                        |          |
|              | Italics     On                         |          |
|              |                                        |          |
|              +----------------------------------------+          |
|              | Press ↵  to change setting - ESC to exit|         |
|              +----------------------------------------+          |
|                                                                  |
|  Choose  ↓↑    Select  ↵              ESC - Go Back              |
+------------------------------------------------------------------+
```

Figure 12-7   Layout options selection window.

to not overdo it, however. Try out different styles to see which looks best for you.

As for the Name Header, you may also opt to either center or left justify the Section Headers.

Sub-Section Headers: It is clearly useful if sub-section headers (such as Major, QPA, Minor, and so on) also stand out on the page. Because it is not a good idea to break up the page too much, you will find the sub-section headers on the same line as the data that accompanies them. To make the header stand out from the data you can use **bold face**, underlining, or *italics,* and you can mix any of them, too. Try all ways in order to find out which you like best.

Line Spacing: This is a very useful feature of THE RESUME WRITER. There is always an advantage to keeping your resume limited to one page. But sometimes you may find that you have just one or two lines that go over onto a second page. The Line Spacing function, available on most printers, enables you to **compress** the text, so that instead of having the standard 66 lines per page you will get 72 lines per page. Try this feature if your resume doesn't quite fit on one page. You may find that it is just what the doctor ordered!

12.4   PREPARING THE PRINTER FOR PRINTING

You should know how to turn on your printer if you are using your own at home. Otherwise, if you are using a printer set up in a school or business environment, it is possible that you may need to do more than simply turn on the power switch. Perhaps the computer you are using is connected to a network that shares a printer. Perhaps the printer is actually in another part of the building, or even in another building altogether.

Local conditions may need local knowledge and help. Thus, if you are using a computer system other than your own, and you are not sure about what to do, get help from someone who uses the system all the time. It will not take you long to learn what you need to know. But it might take forever if you try to figure it out for yourself.

Another problem you might encounter is that of feeding paper into the printer if the supply of paper runs out. You might also run into the problem of paper getting jammed in the feed mechanism of the printer. Such things do happen! This, and other such problems, are best handled by people who work on the spot. They have encountered these and other situations before; they know exactly what to do. You will save yourself significant amounts of time (not to mention significant levels of frustration!) by taking advantage of any help that is in the offing.

When you are ready to print, you will select Print from the Main Menu (Fig. 12-8).

THE RESUME WRITER has been designed to help you with two problems that will always need to be addressed:

1. setting the number of copies of your resume you require;
2. aligning the paper correctly in the printer.

These will be dealt with in the next two sections.

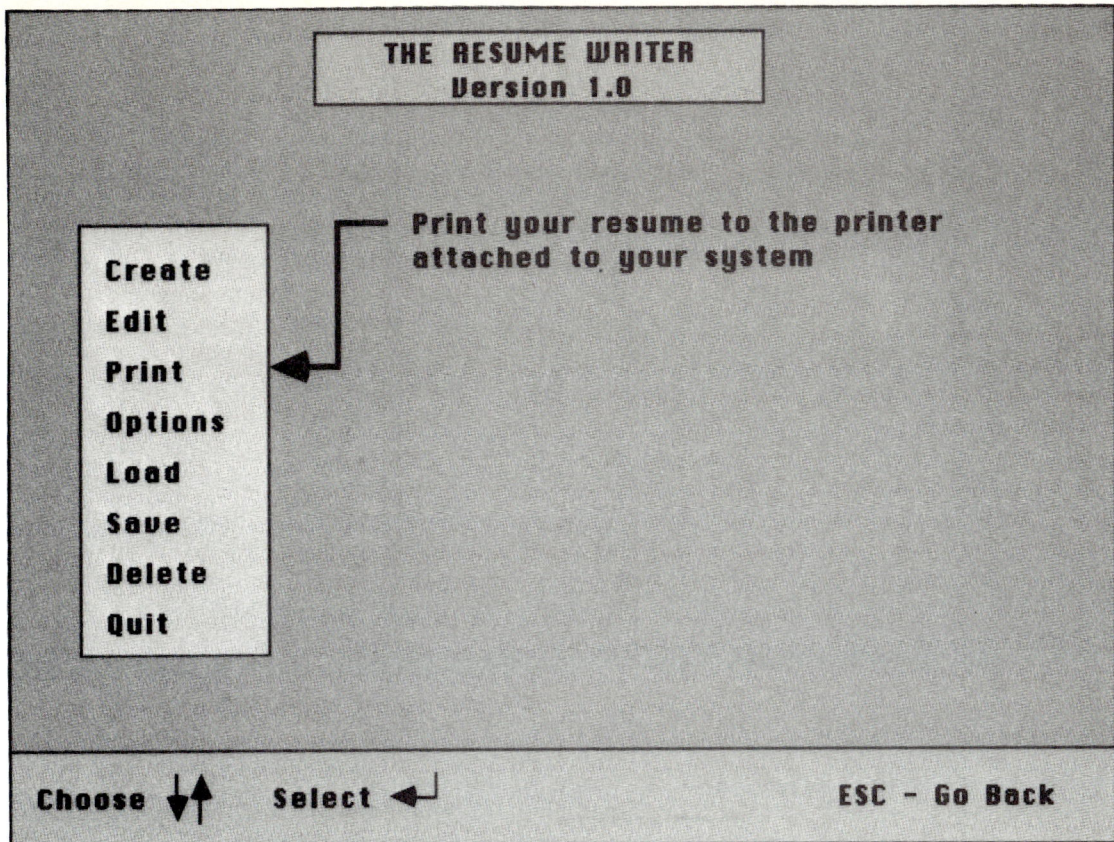

THE RESUME WRITER
Version 1.0

Print your resume to the printer
attached to your system

Create
Edit
Print
Options
Load
Save
Delete
Quit

Choose ↕   Select ←   ESC – Go Back

Figure 12-8 Print option from the main menu.

12.4.1 SETTING THE NUMBER OF COPIES YOU REQUIRE

To do this you will select **Print** from the **Main Menu**, followed by **Number Copies** from the **Print** menu (Fig. 12-9). As you can see in Fig. 12-10, the system will then prompt you for the number of copies that you want to print. You can specify anything up to 99 copies at a time! But would you necessarily want to run off more than one copy of a resume?

The answer to this question depends on the quality of the printer that you are using. The final resume can only be as good as the printer on which it is printed. If the ribbon is old and worn, if the typeface on the printer is cheap or dirty or worn, and if the paper in the printer is low quality, then your resume will be unpresentable. Clearly you would not want to print out 50 copies of your resume off such a printer. It would be a waste of time and money.

On the other hand, in order to get a feel for what the final copy will look like, you might want to turn out just one copy, even off a printer which leaves something to be desired. You would want to experiment with different layouts. Then, once you have the resume the way you want it, you can take THE RESUME WRITER disk with your resume on it to a system with a high quality printer, such as a laser printer, and run off multiple copies there.

One thing is for sure, you would *never* want to send out a final copy of your resume that has been printed on serated-edged computer paper. Photocopying

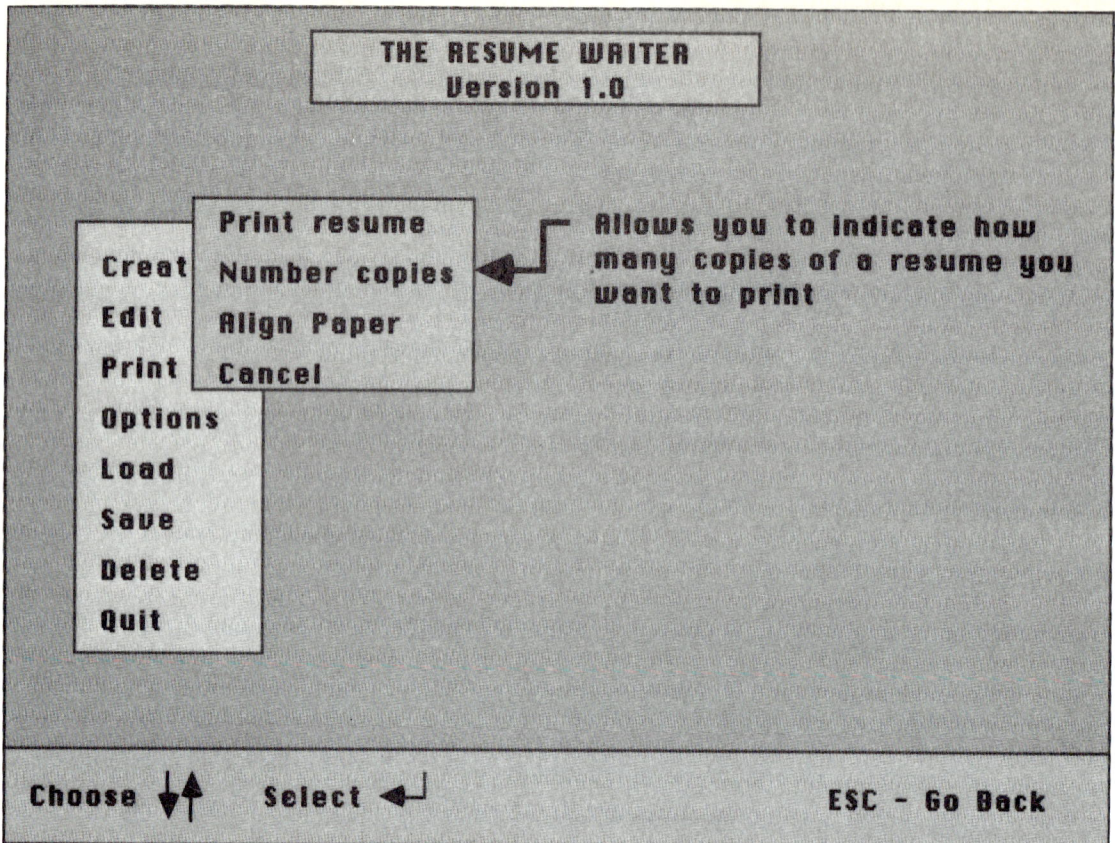

Figure 12-9 Number of copies option from print menu.

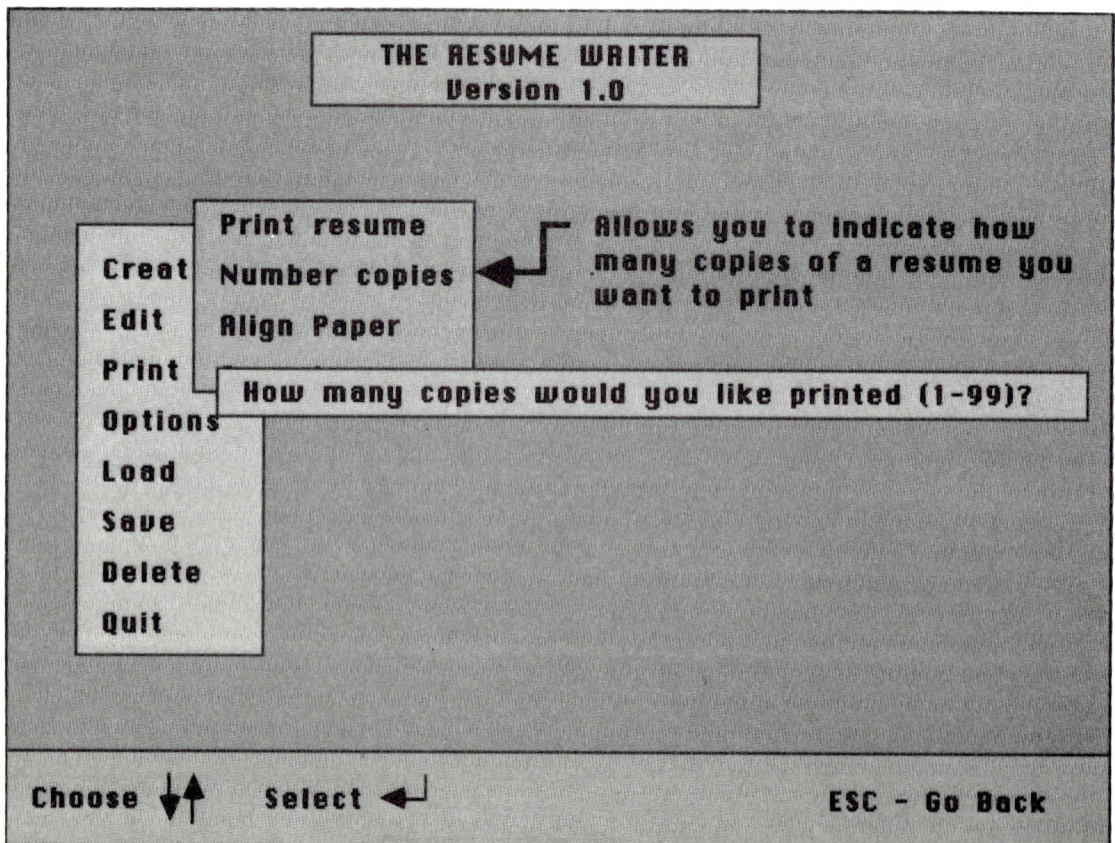

Figure 12-10 Prompt for selecting the number of copies.

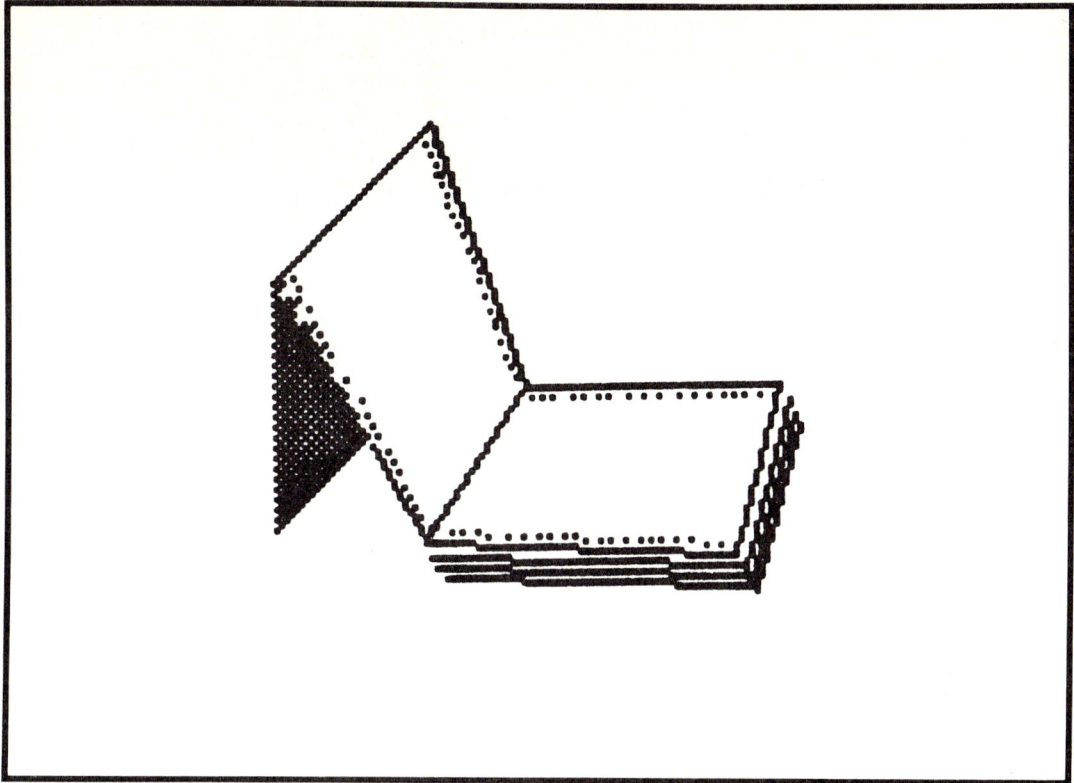

Figure 12-11 Continuous form paper.

machines are such high quality today that sometimes you can actually improve on an original by photocopying it. So if the only printer you have at your disposal is one that prints on continuous form (also called tractor-fed) computer paper of the type illustrated in Fig. 12-11, you should reproduce copies of the resume with a good photocopying machine. You would use one of the kinds of paper recommended in Chapter Two. The cost for this at a professional printing company is no more than a few cents per copy.

Of course, if the printer you have at your disposal is letter quality and able to print one separate page at a time (such as a laser printer), you will be able to produce final copies of your resume for dispersal to prospective employers.

12.4.2 ALIGNING THE PAPER CORRECTLY IN THE PRINTER

You may need to check that you have the paper aligned so that the resume is nicely centered with an appropriate top margin when it is printed out.

In order to check this, you would select **Print** from the **Main Menu** in the usual way. Then you would select **Align Paper** from the **Print** menu (Fig. 12-12). The printer will immediately print a broken line across the page that is set up in the machine.

This broken line represents the position of the serated edge at the very top of the page when it is sent to the printer. Your resume should begin printing about one inch from the top of the page. If necessary, you will have to adjust the paper in the printer until you can guarantee that that is the kind of top margin

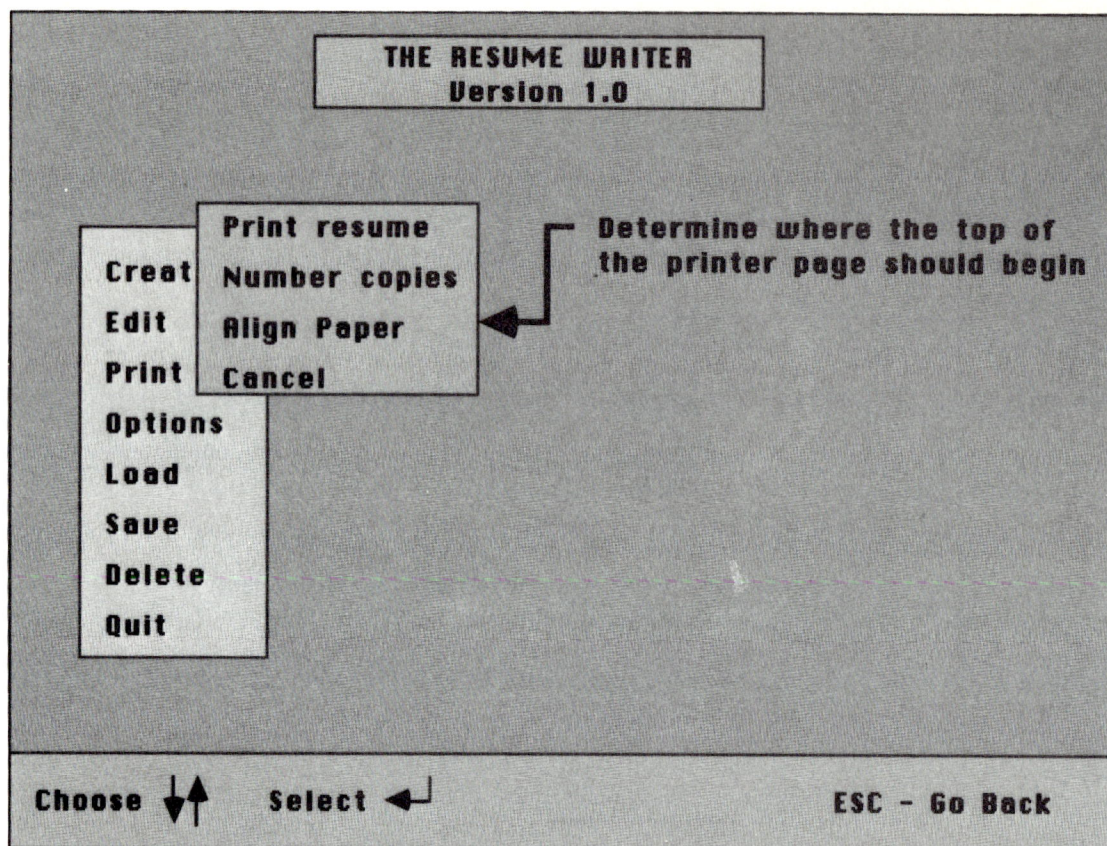

THE RESUME WRITER
Version 1.0

Print resume
Number copies
Align Paper
Cancel

Creat
Edit
Print
Options
Load
Save
Delete
Quit

Determine where the top of
the printer page should begin

Choose ↕   Select ↵   ESC - Go Back

Figure 12-12 Align paper option from the print menu.

you will get. Once set, every page of your resume, if it is more than one page, and every ensuing copy of your resume, will have the same top margin.

12.5 SENDING THE RESUME TO THE PRINTER

You should only send your resume to the printer after you have considered all the page layout and alignment aspects of the finished product.

Actually sending the resume to the printer is simple enough. Select **Print** from the **Main Menu**. This will bring up the **Print menu** from which you will select **Print Resume** (Fig. 12-13).

Providing that you have a good quality printer, specifically one that is clearly capable of producing "letter quality" output, providing, too, that you have applied the recommendations for good resume writing as spelled out in PART I of this book, then the resume that you produce using THE RESUME WRITER will be an effective tool in your job search.

There is always the possibility, however, that you want to take more control of the final product. You like the ease with which THE RESUME WRITER allows you to collect the appropriate data for a good resume. But you have the skills to take advantage of the complete freedom and flexibility of a general word processing environment to specify the layout for the document that will sell you to the world. You are the Power User. You should read on to find out how THE RESUME WRITER has been designed to meet your needs.

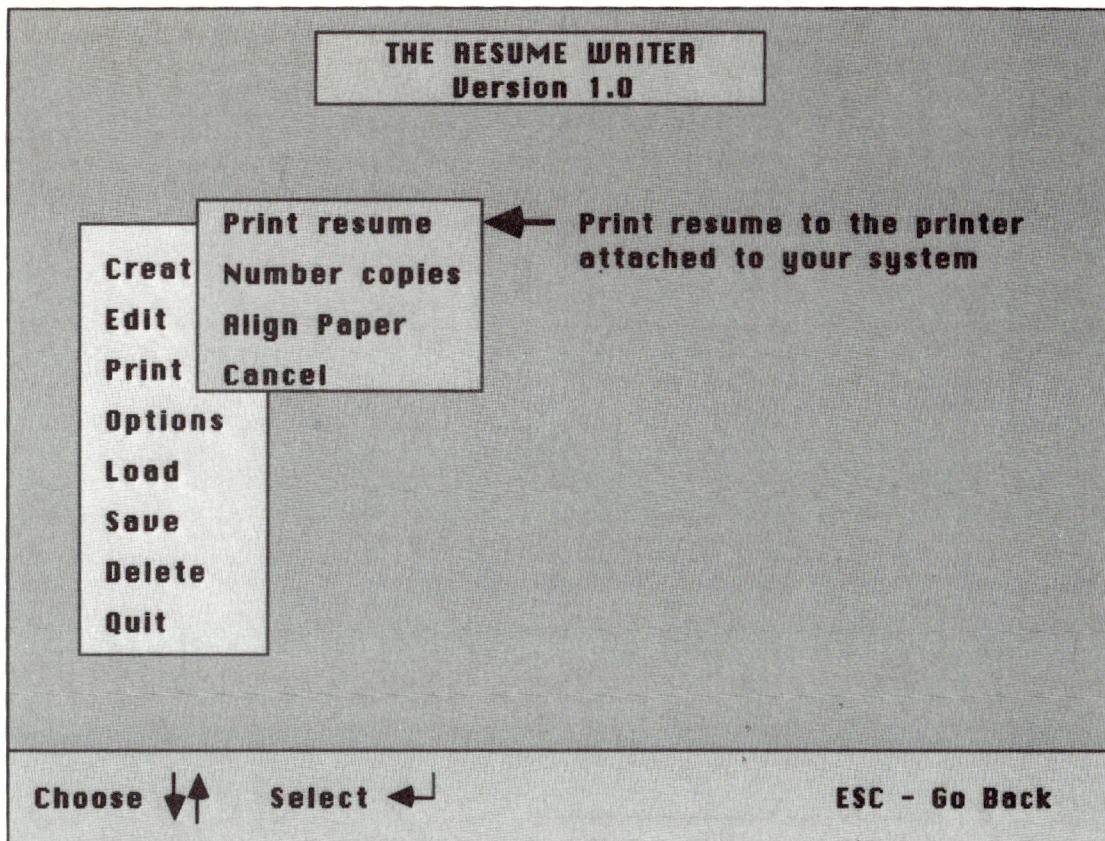

Figure 12-13   Print resume selection from the print menu.

chapter 13

The Power User

LEARNING OBJECTIVES:

As the title of this chapter implies, it is useful reading for the Power User. After reading this chapter you should know whether or not you have enough experience with computers to take advantage of some not so straightforward features of THE RESUME WRITER.

- □ Who is a "Power User?"
- □ Printing (writing) your resume to disk
- □ Loading your resume into a word processor

13.1 WHO IS A POWER USER?

What is meant by "Power User?" Well, you don't have to be a Computer Science major to take advantage of the options explained in this chapter. But you do need to know how to use a word processor, whether on the IBM PC or compatible systems or on other systems such as the Apple Macintosh. This will allow you complete individualized control over the content and layout of your resume once you have gathered the basic data using THE RESUME WRITER.

When you save your resume in the normal way it is saved on your disk as a file that only THE RESUME WRITER can handle.

When, on the other hand, you **Print To Disk**, a feature you select from the **Options** item in the **Main Menu** (Fig. 13-1), you are telling the system to format the file in a way that will make it readable by other word processors. The advantage of this is that it allows you to then take that file and load it into a word processor such as Word Perfect, WordStar, or any one of the many

```
                    ┌─────────────────────────────┐
                    │     THE RESUME WRITER        │
                    │       Version 1.0            │
                    └─────────────────────────────┘



            ┌──────────────┐    ┌─ Change the appearance of your
            │              │    │  resume, select printers, or print
            │  Create      │    │  your resume to a disk file
            │              │    │
            │  Edit        │    │
            │              │    │
            │  Print       │    │
            │              │    │
            │  Options   ◄─┘
            │
            │  Load
            │
            │  Save
            │
            │  Delete
            │
            │  Quit
            │
            └──────────────┘



    Choose  ↓↑     Select  ◄┘                           ESC - Go Back
```

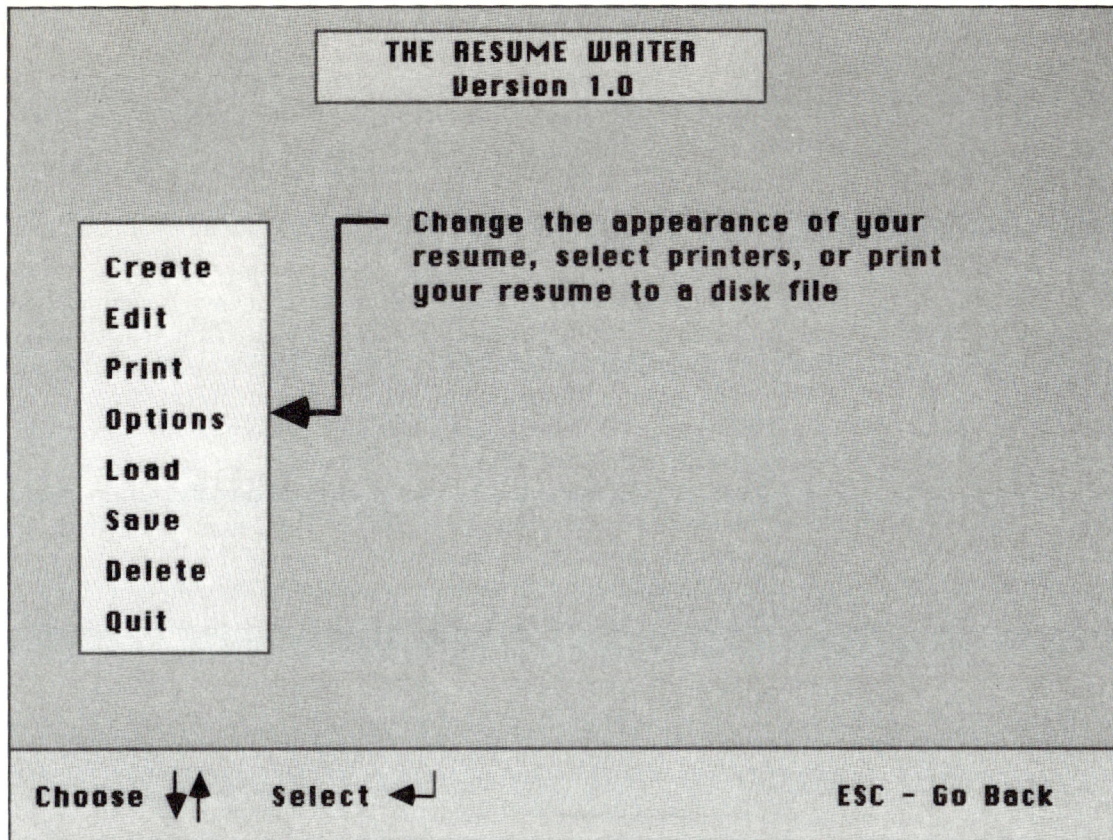

Figure 13-1 Options selection from main menu.

others available that run under MS-DOS on the IBM PC or compatible machines.

THE RESUME WRITER has inherent, and intentional, limitations based on the fact that the software is designed to help those who simply do not know how to begin to put together their resume. The software assumes that you need help selecting the categories of data you will need for your resume. It also assumes you will need help presenting this data in an appropriate sequence. Finally, it assumes you need help laying out your resume.

There is, of course, every reason why even an expert resume writer, such as a career counsellor, might use THE RESUME WRITER as a vehicle for capturing all the detailed data necessary to put together their own, or another's, personal resume. Certainly, a career counsellor might recommend that a client use THE RESUME WRITER for the initial pass at putting together a professional resume. This is akin to what now happens in some doctors' offices or psychotherapists' offices, where the computer is programmed to interact with the patient. The system asks questions, the responses to which provide a provisional profile that can serve as a foundation for diagnosis and eventual cure of a patient's ills.

But a career counsellor, working on his or her own resume, or guiding a client through the process of developing a resume, might well have personal views about how a resume should be displayed on the page, and might therefore find THE RESUME WRITER limiting in this respect. Thus, the option of being able to use a general purpose word processor to customize a resume file collected using THE RESUME WRITER is really quite a powerful idea, which is why it is recommended to the Power User.

A caveat is needed, however. If you do not have a good understanding of what does and does not constitute a quality resume, it is likely that "doing your own thing" will be more of a hindrance than a help. Only take the Power User option of **Printing to Disk** if you are an experienced and successful resume writer.

13.2   PRINTING (WRITING) YOUR RESUME TO DISK

Printing your resume to disk is an alternative to saving your resume on your disk in the normal way. This option is called up by first selecting the **Options Menu** from the **Main Menu** (Fig. 13-1). This brings up a second menu on the screen (the **Options Menu**) from which you select **Print To Disk** (Fig. 13-2).

The system will ask you to name the file that you intend to Print To Disk. This is no different from saving your resume in the normal way. If you are a Power User, you will undoubtedly know how to do this, but just in case, you might like to review the requirements for naming files, and saving them on selected disks, as described in Chapter Ten.

Just one last thing to bear in mind: the extension that THE RESUME WRITER adds to the file name that you come up with under this option will be .TXT, not .RWF as for regular RESUME WRITER files.

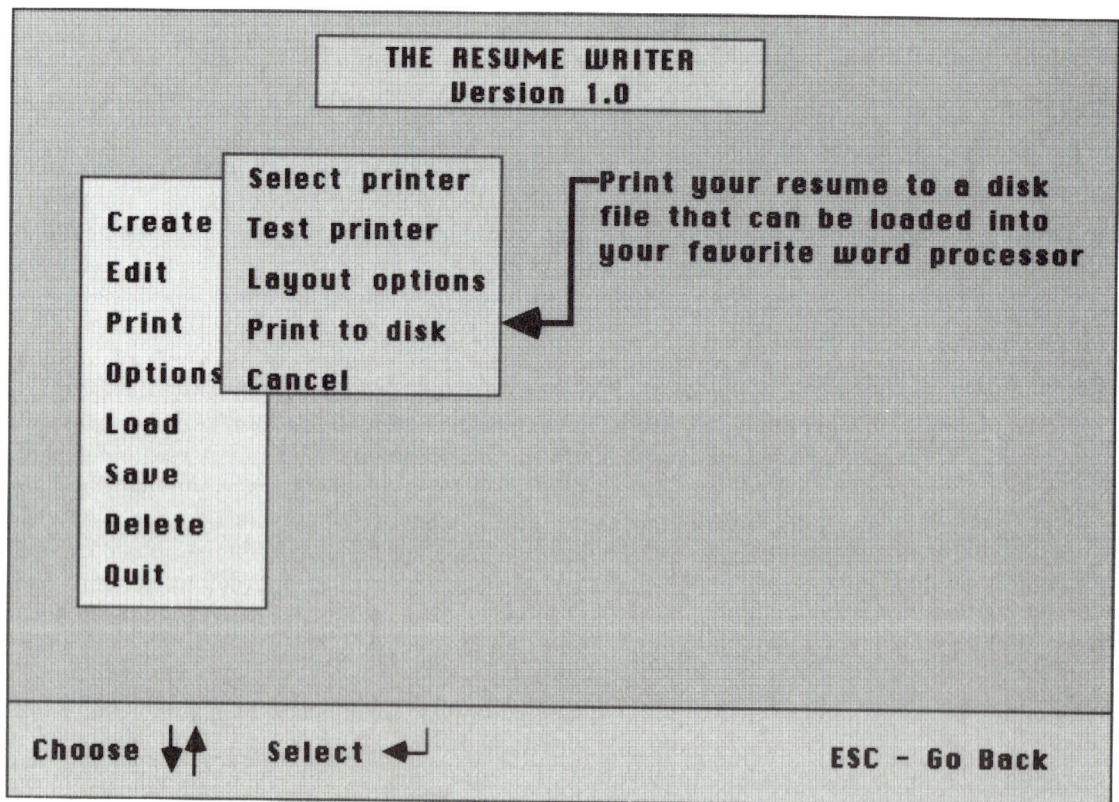

Figure 13-2   Print to disk option from options menu.

13.3 LOADING YOUR RESUME INTO A WORD PROCESSOR

Once you have your resume file Printed To Disk, it will be accessible to any word processor that can handle plain ASCII[1] text files. This is true of just about any word processor in current use.

To transfer your resume file to a computer system other than an IBM PC or compatible machine, you will need to find out what "interfacing" software or even hardware you will need to accomplish this, since the methods for storing data on disks differs from system to system. It is beyond the scope of this book to cover the myriad cases that would apply. The best advice is to check with the company that manufactures your computer system (such as Commodore, or Apple) in order to find out what, if anything, you need to make your system capable of transferring files from and to the IBM PC.

---

[1] ASCII (American Standard Code for Information Interchange) is, as its name implies, a standard code used for transmitting data from computer to computer. Every character on the keyboard, including all the non-alphabetic characters such as punctuation marks, has a unique representation in ASCII code.

What You Need to Know About Computers to Use THE RESUME WRITER

LEARNING OBJECTIVES:

After reading this section you will understand the following facts about microcomputer systems in general and about the IBM PC or PC compatible computers in particular:

□ Minimum system requirements for THE RESUME WRITER
□ What the various parts of the system do
□ What you need to know to use the computer
□ Setting up THE RESUME WRITER diskette with MS-DOS
□ How to begin using THE RESUME WRITER software

A.1 MINIMUM SYSTEM REQUIREMENTS FOR THE RESUME WRITER

As illustrated in Fig. A-1 the various pieces of PC **hardware** that you will need are as follows:

- the system unit
- the monitor
- the keyboard
- the disk drive
- the printer

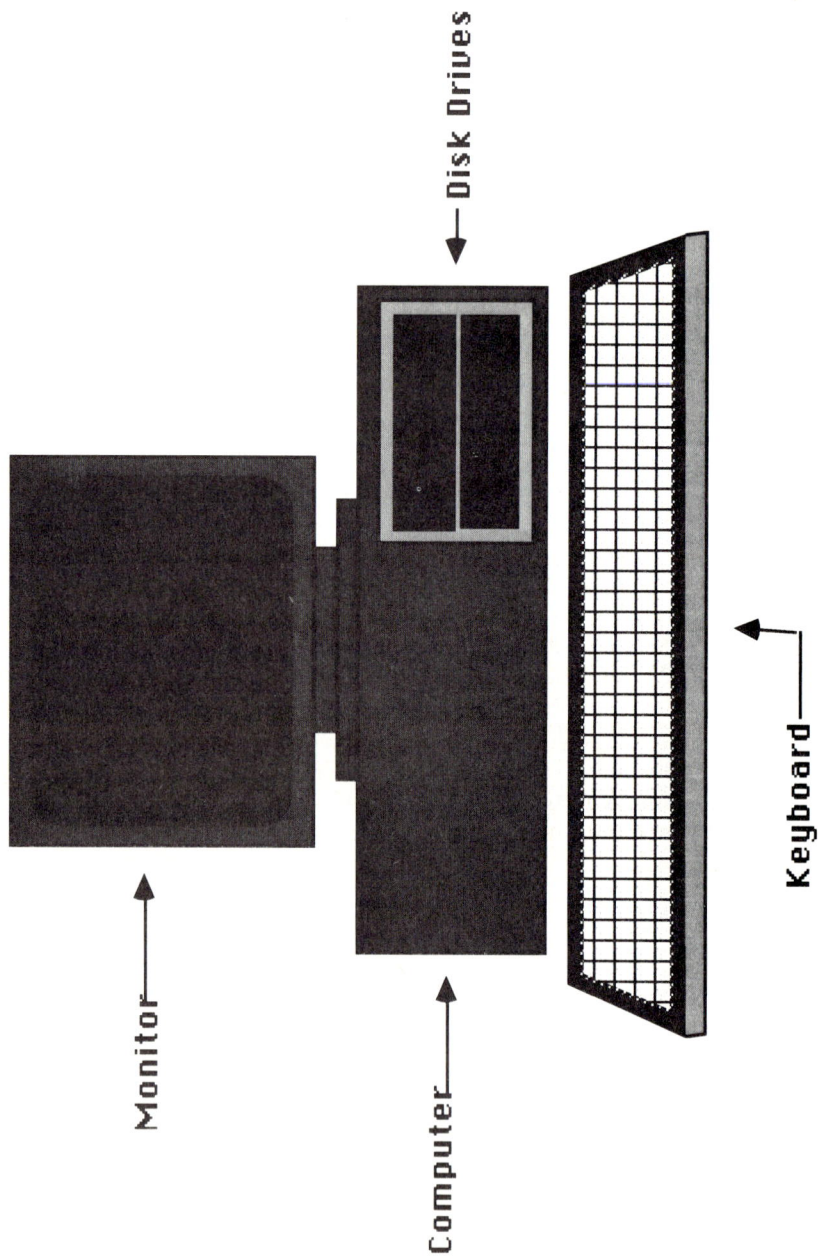

Disk Drives

Monitor

Computer

Keyboard

Figure A-1   Illustration of hardware (not including printer).

112

A.2   WHAT THE VARIOUS PARTS OF THE SYSTEM DO

Let's take them one by one.

A.2.1   THE SYSTEM UNIT

The system unit, which usually sits underneath the monitor, contains the computer chips that control everything that happens while you are working at the computer. You do not need to know anything at all about the electronics involved. Just know that in the unlikely event that the system unit goes down, everything goes down!

The IBM PC or compatible on which you will produce your resume using THE RESUME WRITER should have at least version 2.0 of MS-DOS or PC-DOS. It should also have a minimum 320K of Random Access Memory (RAM). Finally, your system will need to have at least a CGA graphics card installed.

A.2.2   THE MONITOR

If you have not spent much time with computers, you may not be familiar with the term "monitor." In actual fact, the monitor is much like the TV in your home. You'll also hear it described as a VDT (Video Display Terminal), or a CRT (Cathode Ray Tube).

The monitor is used to display what is going on in the system unit of the computer. When you type anything at the keyboard, it will be displayed on the monitor. This is necessary because it keeps you in touch with what is going on in the computer itself. What you see on the monitor reassures you that the system is behaving in a sensible way.

THE RESUME WRITER looks best when run on a color monitor though it will run perfectly well on a monochrome monitor, too. The monochrome monitor is like a black and white TV.

A.2.3   THE KEYBOARD

It is unlikely that you do not know what a keyboard is or what it is used for. With most computer systems, the keyboard is the most important means of getting data into the system so that it can be processed. You will use it to enter the details of your resume.

Fig. A-2 illustrates some important keys on the keyboard which you will need to use and with which you may not be familiar. Compare Fig. A-2 with your own keyboard so that you can locate these keys. They may be marked differently on your keyboard. For example, the key marked ⇐ in Fig. A-2 may have the word "DEL," OR "DELETE," or "BACKSPACE" written on it on your keyboard.

A.2.4   THE DISK DRIVE(S)

You will only need one disk drive to run THE RESUME WRITER. If there are two disk drives on the system that you will be using, you will put THE RESUME WRITER disk in Drive A. As you can see from Fig. A-1, the disk drive(s) is built into the system unit of the computer.

IBM PC Compatible Keyboard

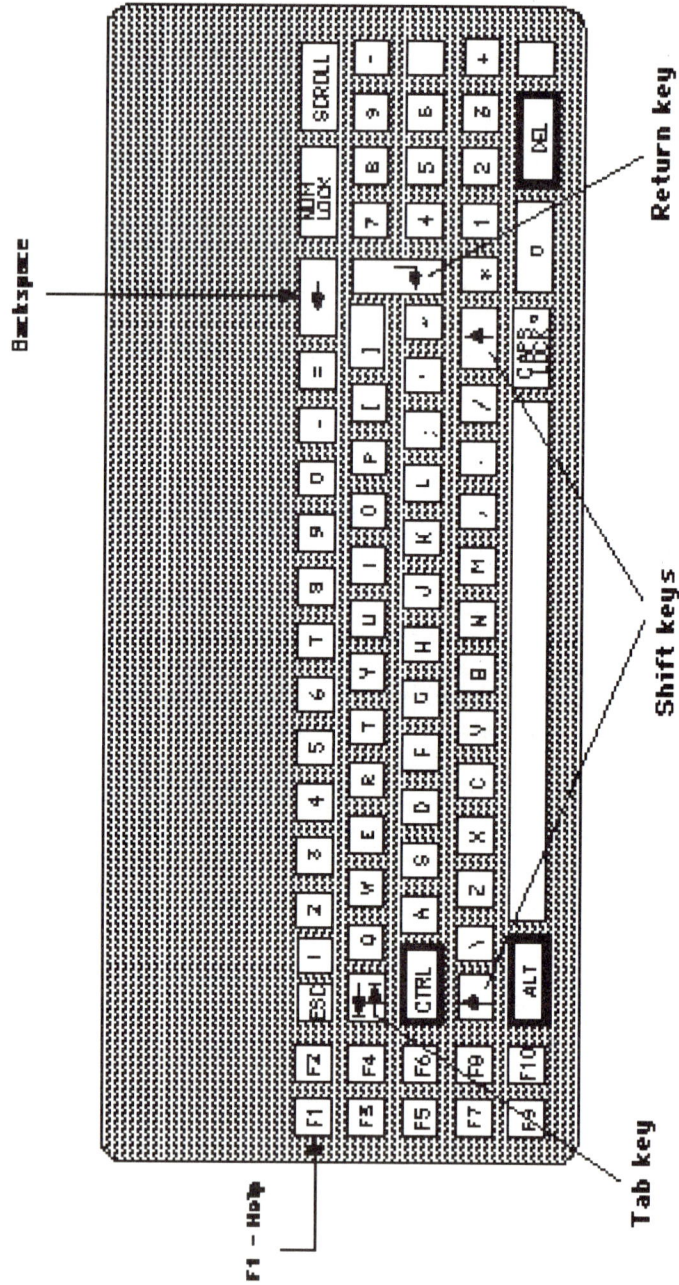

Figure A-2 Close-up of the IBM PC keyboard.

114

The diskette is also categorized as external (or secondary) memory. It is essential that computers have secondary memory because it is the only way to save the work that you have done after the computer is turned off.

When you first create your resume using THE RESUME WRITER you will notice the light come on on the disk drive after you have finished entering all the data. This is a safety precaution. The program is saving your work for you so there is less chance you will lose it.

A.2.5   THE PRINTER

THE RESUME WRITER can be used with a number of different printers. The printer attached to the system which you will be using is probably compatible with one of those for which the program has been specially set up.

Later on, you will be able to check the model of your printer against the list of printers that THE RESUME WRITER recognizes. Should you find that your printer is not one of those that THE RESUME WRITER can work with, don't panic. Read Chapter Twelve to find out how to get around this problem.

The appearance of your resume ultimately depends on the quality of your printer. More to the point, the appearance of your resume ultimately depends on how well your printer has been cared for. Of course, if you have a low quality printer then you can hardly expect to get anything other than low quality results. "You can't make a silk purse from a sow's ear," as the saying goes. But often a printer can be made to look cheap because it is not cared for and also because it is not used correctly.

The ribbon is the easiest component to control. For a few dollars, the purchase of a new ribbon will greatly improve the definition of the type on the printed page.

If you have a choice of computers, use the one that has the best printer. It will not take you long to try out different systems. After you have created your resume you can take THE RESUME WRITER diskette from computer to computer until you find a printer that does a quality job. This is especially convenient if you are a student at a university or college where there may be whole labs full of IBM PC-compatible machines for you to use.

A.3   WHAT YOU NEED TO KNOW TO USE THE COMPUTER

The ensuing sections of Appendix A will help you with the following preliminary tasks:

- how to handle THE RESUME WRITER diskette
- how to put the diskette in the drive
- how to use the printer

A.3.1   HOW TO HANDLE THE RESUME WRITER DISKETTE

The computer diskette that is used to store THE RESUME WRITER can take a certain amount of punishment, but it should nonetheless be handled with care. When not in use, the diskette should always be kept in its protective sleeve (Fig. A-3). This sleeve is specially coated to protect the diskette from static electricity and the like.

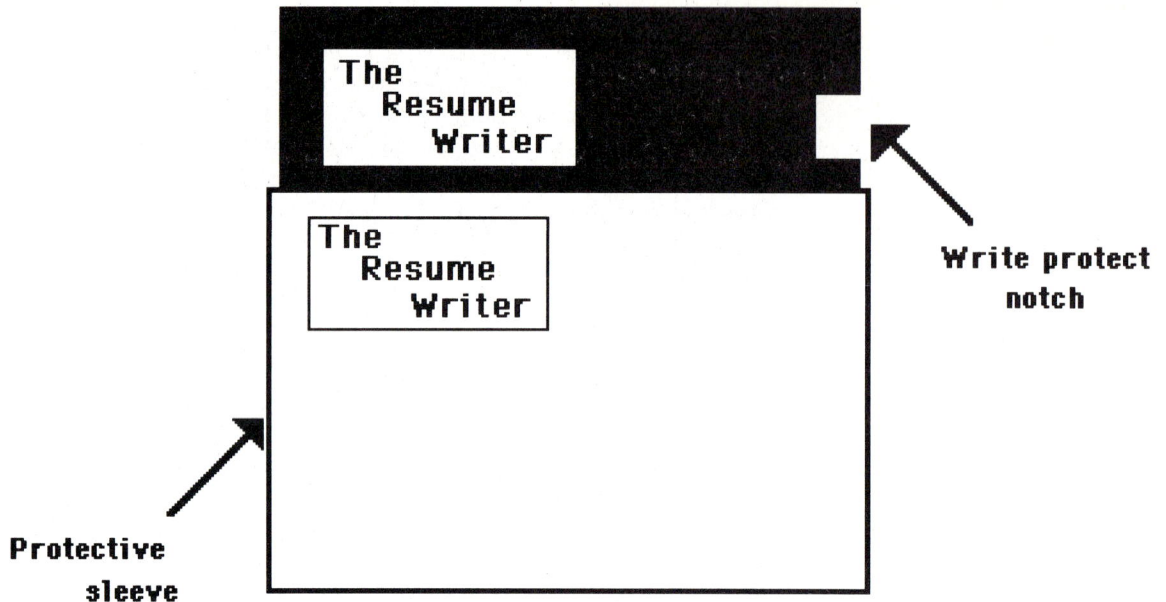

Figure A-3 Diskette in its protective sleeve.

Fig. A-4 shows you how to hold a diskette. With regard to the danger of losing data, you should always protect your diskettes from damage due to extremes of heat or cold, or exposure to liquids or food, especially of the sticky variety. For example, you should not leave your diskettes in your car on either a hot summer's day or on a particularly bone chilling winter's day. Also, never bend or fold the diskette.

When you remove the diskette from the protective sleeve, you will notice that there is a small area cut away (Fig. A-5) which exposes the specially coated plastic disk on which the data is actually stored. Be careful not to touch this one small exposed area, since you could otherwise destroy the data on the disk.

You will need to identify your diskettes by writing names on them. Usually you will write the name of a diskette on the sticker label **before** you attach the label. If you write on the label **after** you have stuck it on the diskette, always do so with a soft, felt-tip marker (Fig. A-6).

Fig. A-7 illustrates that there is a correct and an incorrect orientation of the diskette when you put it in the disk drive. If you examine the diskette, you will see that one side (the reverse side) has folds along the edges where the outer casing of the diskette has been stuck down. The other side of the diskette is entirely smooth along the edges. The smooth side is the front side, and should always be facing up when you put the diskette into the disk drive.

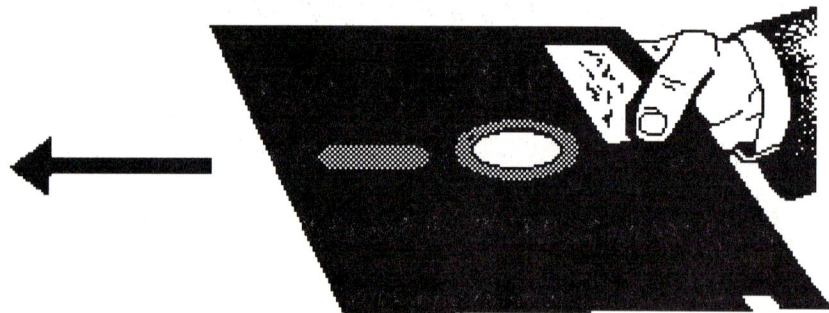

Figure A-4 Handling a diskette.

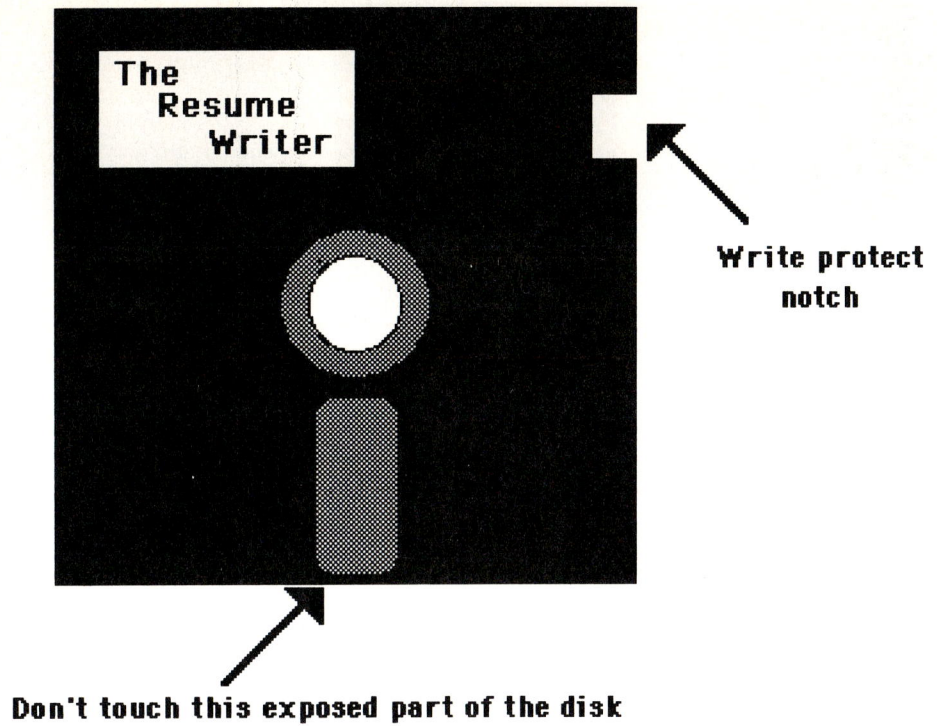

Write protect notch

Don't touch this exposed part of the disk

Figure A-5 Taking care of the diskette.

Figure A-6 Don't write on a diskette with a ball-point pen or pencil.

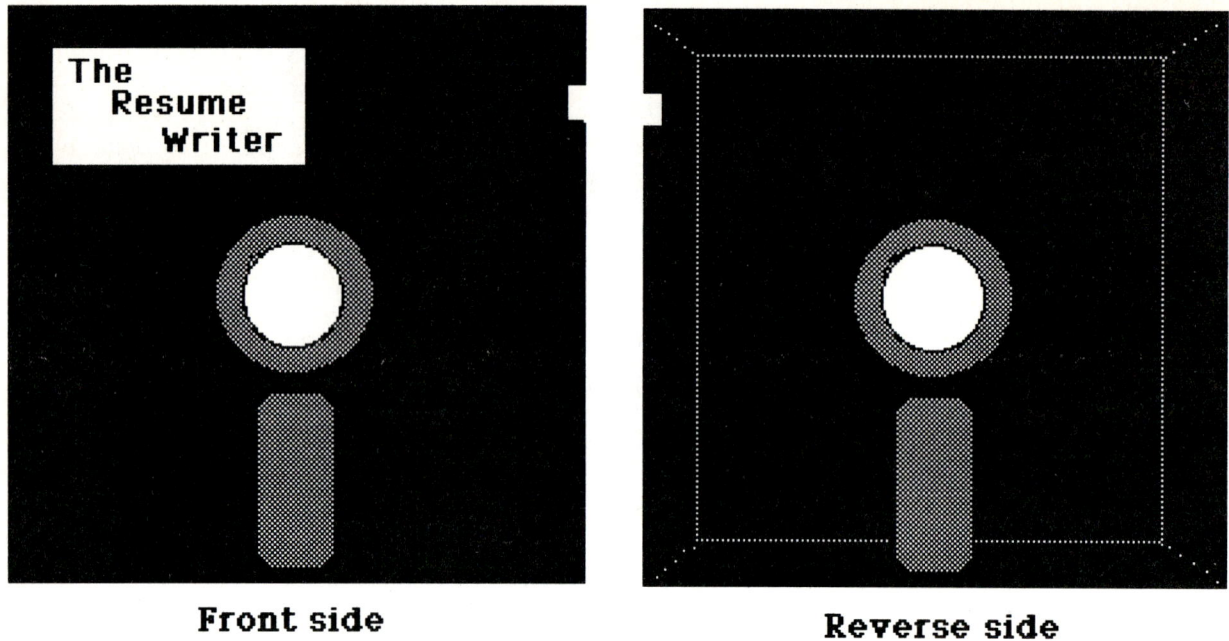

Front side   **Reverse side**

Figure A-7 Front and reverse side of diskette.

A.3.2 HOW TO PUT THE DISKETTE IN THE DISK DRIVE

There is a lever, or "door" as it is called, that closes over the slot in the disk drive where the diskette goes. This door should be open when you put the diskette into the disk drive. Holding the diskette as illustrated in Fig. A-5, gently slide the diskette into the disk drive. Never force the diskette into place. Once the diskette is fully inserted into the drive, close the door.

When you are done working with THE RESUME WRITER, remove the diskette by opening the door and gently sliding out the diskette. Be sure to replace the diskette in its protective sleeve.

A.3.3 HOW TO USE THE PRINTER

Because there are so many different types of printers, it will be impossible to explain how to use them all in this manual. However, certain general rules apply. On the whole THE RESUME WRITER helps you to successfully print your resume on the printer attached to your system. It does this by showing you how to align the paper so that the resume begins toward the top of the page. THE RESUME WRITER will also help you to select type characteristics and page layouts for different parts of your resume. This is explained in Chapter Twelve.

But you will have to experiment with your printer in order to learn how to put in the paper, how to take it out, how to change the ribbon, how to turn the printer on and off, how to adjust the page, and so on. If you are using your own system, you will no doubt have already figured out all these details. But if using computers is a new experience for you, or you are using a system with which you are not familiar, you will need to get someone to show you what to do.

A.4   SETTING UP THE RESUME WRITER DISKETTE WITH MS-DOS

If your system does not have a hard disk drive, the most convenient set up is to install the MS-DOS operating system on the same diskette as THE RESUME WRITER software. The advantage of this is that whenever you want to use THE RESUME WRITER it will be much more straightforward to "boot" the software.

Consult your MS-DOS user manual to see how to format a self-booting disk. Then copy all the files from THE RESUME WRITER master disk onto the newly formatted self-booting disk.

A.5   HOW TO BEGIN USING THE RESUME WRITER SOFTWARE

This is really very simple. If the computer system is not already switched on, turn on the system. The switch is usually at the back of the system unit (see Fig. A-1).

If the computer system is already switched on, but you do not see the system prompt reset the system by simultaneously pressing the **control** key, the **alt** key, and the **delete** key (see Fig. A-8).

Once the system is booted, follow these simple directions:

If you DO NOT have a hard disk drive with your system

1. Put THE RESUME WRITER diskette in Drive A.
2. Type **RW** and press the **Return** key.
3. Wait while THE RESUME WRITER is booted.

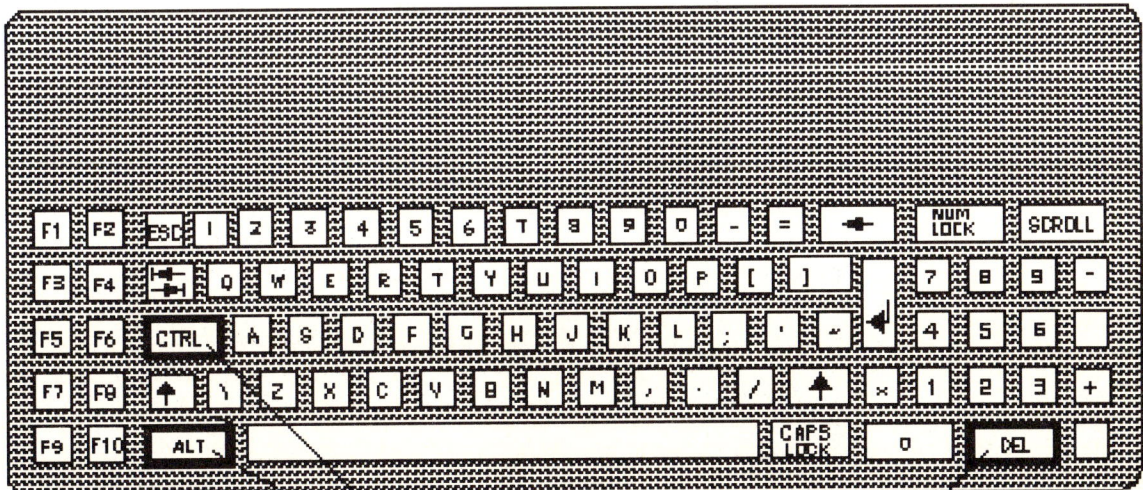

Hold down these two keys...   then press this key

Figure A-8   Location of keys to reset the system.

If you DO have a hard disk drive with your system, THE RESUME WRITER can be installed on your hard drive. In fact, if you have your own system, you will undoubtedly know how to do this, and have probably already done so. In this case, all you need to do to run THE RESUME WRITER is to type:

c:\RW

unless you have opened a special directory for THE RESUME WRITER on your hard disk, in which case you would specify the appropriate complete path name.

Once installed on your hard disk drive, THE RESUME WRITER will save all versions of your resume in the same directory as the software itself. This makes sense, since your resumes created with the help of THE RESUME WRITER should be stored along with it.

If you have not already done so, it would not be a bad idea to set up a special directory for THE RESUME WRITER on your hard disk. Then you will always know where the relevant files are, and they won't be mixed in with the other documents and programs stored in your system.

It's always best to set up a directory like this straight away. Why? Because it will be much more difficult to do so later, since you may have files all over the place. Use the **Mkdir** command in MS-DOS to create a new directory with the name of your choice. If you have your own system with a hard disk drive, you should already know how to do this.

Glossary

Apple: Apple Computer Corporation, manufacturer of top-selling Apple II and Macintosh microcomputer families.

Arithmetic Unit: Part of the CPU which handles all mathematical processing done by the computer system.

ASCII Code: American Standard Code for Information Interchange—used to represent up to 256 different characters (letters of the alphabet, and so on) in the 1's and 0's of Machine Language.

Auxilliary Storage: See Secondary Storage.

Backup: A copy of your data, made in case of loss.

Bit: Short for **BI**nary Digi**T**, i.e. a 1 (one) or a 0 (zero) in Machine Language.

Boot: Activate, or start up, a computer system (hardware or software).

Byte: A collection of Bits (usually 7, 8, or 9 bits); each byte represents in the computer a character (letter of the alphabet, digit, punctuation, and so forth).

Cathode Ray Tube: See Monitor.

Central Processing Unit: The "brain" of the computer; it contains the logic, or instructions, that control everything that goes on in the computer system.

Chip: A small slice of silicon (about 1/4 inch square) on which are layered electronic circuits and switches which are the fundamental components of a computer system.

Chronological resume: A resume format style which presents a reverse chronological listing of experience and education and draws attention to dates. Most recent experiences are listed first.

Combination resume: A resume format style which combines a summary of skills and qualifications with a chronological history of employment and/or education.

Control Unit: The part of the CPU which "controls" the execution of each instruction given to the computer.

CPU: See Central Processing Unit.

CRT: See Cathode Ray Tube.

Delete a file: Remove a file from your diskette.

Disk Drive: Secondary Storage device which writes data to, and reads data from, the diskettes.

Diskette: The thin circular disk of metal-coated plastic on which data is electromagnetically stored by the computer.

Drive A: The external disk drive most frequently used for Secondary Storage; it is the drive in which you put THE RESUME WRITER diskette.

Drive B: A second external disk drive often available on microcomputers; useful for your own backup diskette.

External Storage: See Secondary Storage.

Floppy disk: See Diskette.

Floppy disk drive: See Disk Drive.

Fonts: Different styles for the characters that are used for our written language (italics, bold face, and so on).

Format: The general organization of information presented in a resume.

Formats: Any one of the three resume types (see Chronological, Combination, Functional resume).

Freeform Section: Data entry area in THE RESUME WRITER which allows you freedom to layout the text to suit your own preference.

Functional resume: A resume format style which focuses on professional skills and de-emphasizes when, how, or where they were acquired or developed.

Hard Boot: Using the power switch to start up the computer system.

Hard disk drive: Internal disk drive; capable of much greater storage capacity and data access speed than external disk drives (see Disk Drive).

Hardware: The parts of a computer system you can see and touch (the Monitor, Printer, Keyboard, System Unit, and so forth).

IBM PC: The Personal Computer system formerly manufactured by IBM (1981–1987), and now produced as PC-Compatibles by other manufacturers.

Input: Data that is brought into Primary Storage for processing by the computer.

Internal Storage: See Primary Storage.

K: See Kilobyte.

Keyboard: The most commonly used Input device.

Kilobyte: 1024 bytes (2^{10} bytes).

Layout: The way you arrange your resume on the page (use of white space, centering, and so on).

Load a file: Cause the computer to bring a file of data (such as one of your resumes) into Primary Storage from the diskette.

Logic Unit: The unit of the CPU which handles all instructions that have to do with decisionmaking; for example, if you select anything from one of the menus, you are telling the computer to make a decision (see Menu).

Machine Language: The only language the computer understands; it is made up of 1's and 0's (Bits) which are grouped into Bytes and Instructions which tell the computer what to do.

Magnetic disk: See diskette.

Magnetic tape: A Secondary Storage medium used today only with larger computer systems; rarely used with microcomputers.

Menu: A list of choices which allow you to select what you want to do next in THE RESUME WRITER.

Menu-driven: See menu.

Microprocessor: Another name for a CPU; when the first microprocessor was invented in 1971 by Intel Corporation, it was nicknamed "a computer on a chip."

Monitor: The most common display device for computer systems; it is similar to your TV set; used to produce softcopy output (on screen).

Monochrome Monitor: Describes two-tone monitors (black-on-white, or orange-on-black, or white-on-blue, green-on-black, etc.).

MS-DOS: **M**icro**S**oft-**D**isk **O**perating **S**ystem; the most popular operating system controlling IBM PCs; you need version 2.0 or beyond of MS-DOS to use THE RESUME WRITER.

Output: Data that is produced by the computer and transmitted to some kind of output device, such as a Monitor, or Disk Drive, or Printer.

Path name: The route through the files that you have stored on your diskette; you might have your files set up in what MS-DOS calls Directories; then you could have Directories within Directories, and in order to get at them you would have to spell out the path to the system (consult your MS-DOS manual if you are keen to learn more about this).

PC: See IBM PC.

PC Compatible: A computer system which to all intents and purposes is the same as the IBM PC.

PC-DOS: Proprietary IBM version of MS-DOS (see MS-DOS).

Power User: One who has considerable experience using computers in general and, for the purposes of THE RESUME WRITER, the IBM PC or compatibles in particular.

Primary Storage: The memory component of the computer system which is used to temporarily store THE RESUME WRITER software and the resume that you are actually working on at any one time; when you turn off the computer, Primary Storage is erased, which is why you need Secondary Storage such as diskettes on which to save your work when you are done.

Printer: The second most common output device used with computer systems; used to produce hardcopy output (on paper).

Printer ribbon: Same as a typewriter ribbon; it is very important that you keep this well-inked; the better the ribbon, the better your resume will look.

Printer codes: Sequences of ESCape characters used by printers to control the fonts and layout of printed output.

RAM: See Primary Storage.

Resume: A concise, written, directed communication that presents one's accomplishments and demonstrates ability to produce results.

Rough Draft: An outline of the data you need to produce your resume; it is always best to prepare one of these before using THE RESUME WRITER.

Save a file: Tell the computer to make a copy of your resume on the diskette after you are done creating or updating it.

Secondary Storage: Permanent storage for your resumes and for THE RESUME WRITER; usually on a diskette.

Soft Boot: A way of booting the computer when the power switch is already turned **on**; it is done by pressing the RESET button, or by simultaneously pressing Ctrl-Alt-Del buttons on the keyboard; the less you use the power switch the better as far as the computer is concerned.

Software: Computer programs, i.e., the sets of instructions that tell the computer what to do; THE RESUME WRITER is an example of a piece of software.

System Unit: The system unit is the box that contains the microprocessor and other support chips and electronic circuitry which are at the heart of your computer system; it usually resides underneath the Monitor.

VDT: Video Display Terminal (See Monitor).

Annotated Bibliography

More detailed information on, and examples of, resumes can be found in the following references:

CAMDEN, THOMAS M., THE JOB HUNTER'S FINAL EXAM, Surrey Books, Chicago, IL, 1984. A "True/False" test with answers to job hunters' 100 toughest questions.

KRANNICH, RONALD L., WILLIAM J. BANIS, HIGH IMPACT RESUMES AND LETTERS: HOW TO COMMUNICATE YOUR QUALIFICATIONS TO EMPLOYERS, Impact Publications, Manassas, VA, 1988. A guide for every stage of the writing and distribution process.

MEYERS, HOWARD, RESUME PREPARATION, College Placement Council Foundation, Bethlehem, PA, 1986. A guide for resume writing instruction developed to provide professionals with a systematic approach to resume writing.

SUKIENNIK, DIANE, LISA RAUFMAN, WILLIAM BENDAT, THE CAREER FITNESS PROGRAM: EXERCISING YOUR OPTIONS. Gorsuch Scarisbrick, Scottsdale, AZ, 1986. A thorough program for career planning and job search, combining theory with exercises.

YATE, MARTIN JOHN, RESUMES THAT KNOCK 'EM DEAD, Bob Adams, Inc., Boston, MA, 1988. Authoritative advice on the task of composing a resume, written with input from the nation's top personnel, management, and employment specialists.

Index